ఴ

THE OTHER SIDE *of* TUSCANY

ఴ

N. A. STOLFO CORTI

Dearest Kimberly,

Yes, my life is a Country Song, I hope you enjoy "listening" as much as I did to your songs.

THE OTHER SIDE *of* TUSCANY

Warmly,
The Wine Fairy
(Nancy JoontMXIX)

2.23.23
Raleigh, NC

Copyright 2009, 2010 by Nancy Stolfo Corti.

Proof: November 2009, Lulu, Raleigh, North Carolina
First Edition: December 2009, Lulu, Raleigh, North Carolina
CS Edition: January 2010, CreateSpace, Raleigh, North
Carolina

No part of this publication may be reproduced, stored in a
retrieval system, or transmitted in any form or by any means,
electronic, mechanical, photocopying, recording, scanning, or
otherwise, except as permitted under Sections 107 and 109 of
the 1976 United States Copyright Act, without either the prior
written permission of the Publisher or authorization through
payment of the appropriate per-copy fee to the Publisher.

ISBN 10 1449997333
ISBN 13 9781449997335

Requests for publisher Permissions should be addressed to
Permission, ClearSight Creative Resources, 133 Sharp Top
Trail, Apex, NC 27502. 828.398.0390, e-mail
anora@clearsightcreativeresources.com

Printed on Lulu size 6x9.
Font: Times New Roman 12, 11, 10
Chapter Heading Font: Vivaldi 14

All songs are reprinted by permission or in the public domain.

Dedication

This book is dedicated to those of you who have taught a soul to sing, given music to the dance and who have saved friends from themselves. You are the first to arrive; before we even know there is a crisis; you have shed our tears when we have none left to cry. Without you, the angels who walk the earth, this book and my life would not have been possible.

Thank you.

Please visit my blog to know more about these angels, some no longer on this earth.

http://nancystolfocorti.wordpress.com

Website:www.nancystolfocorti.com

Chapters

Chapter 1: The Looking Glass 1

Chapter 2: Just a Little Girl 5

Chapter 3: Rules... 10

Chapter 4: Leaving 17

Chapter 5: The Cost of Protection............................ 22

Chapter 6: Behind Gates.. 26

Chapter 7: Spoils of Gucci....................................... 32

Chapter 8: Customs Cancer 38

Chapter 9: The Iron Curtain 42

Chapter 10: Straddling the Chasm............................ 45

Chapter 11: Marriage... 50

Chapter 12: Forest Friends 58

Chapter 13: Malia 62

Chapter 14: Fear, A Good Thing............................... 68

Chapter 15: Michele... 72

Chapter 16: First Step Out 79

Chapter 17: The Cross We bear 84

Chapter 18: Finding Pictures.................................... 91

Chapter 19: Heart Language 100

Chapter 20: Counting in Black and White 107

Chapter 21: Sister's Grace 113

Chapter 22: Time to Move On 118

Chapter 23: Crossed Lines 129

Chapter 24: Danger 133

Chapter 25: Face to Face 146

Chapter 26: Dream Summons 157

Chapter 27: Forgiveness 167

Chapter 28: What's in a Letter 176

Chapter 29: Lust 185

Chapter 30: Cleansing...189

Chapter 31: Too Close to Home...................................197

Chapter 32: House of Madness 202

Chapter 33: Lemons and Elephants...........................206

Chapter 34: Of Sons & Dogs.......................................210

Chapter 35: Sorrow...218

Chapter 36: Treasured Things 221

Chapter 37: Stay..226

Original Words to Songs in this Book 237

Quotes 245

Locations..249

Who's Who...251

About the Author..252

The brightest future almost always
has a forgotten past, once you let
go, you will rise like the delicate
bubbles of the stomped grapes in
your glass.

~Nac

Chapter 1: The Looking Glass

Gli Scopeti, Tuscany, Italy

I want to remember my life in sequence, but I can't.

I remember smells and sensations. I remember the
way the children were dressed. I remember the way
we made love that afternoon but I cannot tell you
when or where, if we were happy or if we were
fighting.

I cannot tell you what year it was but I can tell you
that in the pit of my stomach I was afraid – I was
always afraid of him and of losing him. I was afraid
of being caught in a Tuscan countryside forgotten
by the rest of the world. Yet I lived in Tuscany
ready to gather guests every summer and poppies
every spring; free to enjoy Tuscany through the
eyes of its visitors but not free to enjoy it myself,
encased as I was in a personal hell of
misunderstanding.

As I walk around my house I see a beautiful rustic
home - my home. Yet, I do not feel as if it is mine
nor that I will ever "hold" it. I felt the same way
when my son Benji was born. They whisked him

away - the child we so desperately tried to bring into this world. The other twin cried out for him but he was gone - no name, no son, no answers to my desperate questions just the tugging of dull thread through my tender flesh as they stitched fervently to stop the hemorrhaging. When I would think back to that moment I would wince not from the pain of the stitching but from the longing in my heart for the tiny son who was taken away from me; away from the protection and safety of his mother.

I look at my home much the same way as I looked at him that first time I had seen him in that tiny glass box fighting for his life. I look at my home as I would a child I wanted to hold in my arms only to be separated with a glass barrier. And like that day I saw my son, when my tears fell upon the glass that held what was so precious to me - I make a vow, "I will hold you. I will have you. I will protect you."

Ironically, the same resolve I made to my husband when I knew he was trying to escape her.

I am sad to say, the last great picture I have of my husband is with another woman; and the last great picture he has of me was taken by another man.

You can see love in the pictures of me, taken by my children and their friends. They capture this woman they love. They capture me; something my husband says he could never do. The images are of appreciation - not a souvenir of an event or of a life I knew nothing about; a life I knew nothing about until I tried to escape mine. How many more of these photographs are there? How many memories and vacations and nights of never-ending sex do I not know about?

❧ The Other Side of Tuscany ☙

When I first found out about *her,* Eleajora, my husband and I chatted like two fraternity brothers discussing a new classmate. He described her mechanically, factual without compliment or criticism: blond, blue-eyed, leggy but short, big breasts and perfect - except for a very flat ass.

"I don't *love* her and I have never said that, except once because I felt guilty."

He concluded the description, almost like giving details to a police officer doing a report after a crime. I did not think that was so bad, after all, I had had affairs too and it was merely for the sex. My problem was everyone seemed to want to have a relationship afterward and I certainly did not have the time or energy. Where were those casual sex partners of my youth?

It was when my husband confided in me that they had made love 89 times one August while they were on vacation, that it hit me. No, not just "hit me" and I am sure there must be a verb that describes this in some language but my language was void of a word that could mean so much hurt in one utterance. They were not on vacation, they were playing house in my house. Making love on my bed. Lighting fires in my hearth. Making pizzas in my wood burning oven.

Who was she to open the book called *my life* and become a chapter?

We - his children and I, struggled every day in America with his absence, his loneliness and the guilt that came with it all. I felt like a forgotten paperback on the nightstand; one that you read with passion until you just fell out of interest after many late nights reading. Here I was in the prime of my life- alone; the fruits of my labor enjoyed by someone else, the luxury of time with my husband consumed by a person I did not even know. What had seemed so easy to walk away from now was tangled about my ankles. I felt a slow anger and self-pity.

They tell you not to marry the man you can live with but to marry the one you cannot live without.

I guess I was only following directions.

We can never live in the past as if it were our true home...It is a good thing that God draws this veil over the past even without our asking. In so doing, he allows us to live today and for tomorrow with just the few memories we need of what was.

~Karl Barth

Chapter 2: Just a Little Girl

Dayton, Ohio, USA 1963

I don't know why I was always kept indoors; if it was because I was still so young I could not play with the others or if it was that I was so accident-prone it was thought safer that way, the fact is most of the world I saw was from behind a glass barrier, my window.

I remember the swing set toppling over and pinning my chubby three year old leg. The black and white 4" x 4" photo, with a yellowing white border, confirming that Gian was there moments before. In jumping off, after swinging high and long, he had caused the lightweight aluminum structure to rock a few times, lurch as if walking, and then dangerously fall. The remaining passenger, thrown like a rag doll into the air with unplanned, simultaneous slow motion, leaving me pinned beneath.

It seemed terrifying to those that witnessed the scene but I had that confidence that somehow, someone was protecting me and nothing serious would really happen. Smiling I peered from beneath the structure and only cried when I saw the oval of worried adults looking down at me.

One Christmas night 21 years later, the celestial hand that kept the swing set from breaking my neck held me and my infant Kikka from crashing through our Mercedes windshield and into the Chianti stream that fed the Greve River near our home in Tuscany. That night, what I knew as a small child in the responsibility of the fixing and the wonder of the creating - was confirmed -that I was special beyond black and white.

Children float through childhood with the laughter and carelessness as a song bird in flight; much is the time but swiftly also is the passing. I pondered childhood as if a great question to be solved. From the earliest memory to the fleeing moments at recess and into adolescence, I worked on the equation and with an underlying uneasiness and I wondered if I was getting it right.

My ally, my brother Gian never understood the shadows that followed me through childhood and then life. He was a songbird, light and carefree through our days, trying to pull me into a simplicity in which I did not belong. We were always together in those early days. Later, in our separation, that togetherness remained and we would will life from one to the other as candles in the church can light each other with the whispers of widows' prayers.

My mother often cried. It would be a letter or a phone call, or the Avon lady who had come to the door; my mom defiant would turn her away yet secretly want the samples and smells of the pale turquoise vanity case.

One day, I do remember she let her in but it never happened again as the miniature lipstick samples found their way to the carpet, my chenille bedspread and the "Sunday" dress that Zia Maria made for me.

It is not that I was a bad child; "Argento Vivo" Nonno Vito had described me, telling my mom not to worry that I would grow out of it. My mother, careful and neat, was frustrated by the creative energy that escaped my every pore and kept her scrambling to right the house every night before my father or Uncle Dan got home. I felt her tears were my fault and something I was doing was making her very sad. Guilt, a genetic necessity, finds safe harbor with our people and I was no exception.

Guilt provided a barrier between my mother and me. Almost as if she could not get close to me, almost as if she were afraid of this child wise beyond her years, who never slept and stood by her parents bed in the middle of the night just to make sure they were still alive.

"What are you doing!?! Go back to bed," my startled mother would say out of breath from the fright I had given her.

In the silence of the night my father would leave for a bakery work bench or a hotel kitchen. Though he moved with the silence of a mouse, I would awaken and stand by my parent's bed until my mother would roll over and wake up. I frightened my mother but what she did not know was that in my room my dreams were waiting and taunting me; robbing me of the peace that most children find in the solace of their naps and bedtime. I, instead, had the questions and the sounds of a life that was laid in a memory not mine.

The dreams were of a beautiful land of fields of wheat and poppies, vineyards and horses - sometimes woven into fabric. There were majestic mountains, rocky beaches and endless canals flowing in and out of focus like fine curtains in the breeze. The dream always ended the same, my mother and I in a wheat field, each tied to our own stake in front of a single oak tree. The moments of peace and beauty were replaced by despair and solitude so thick that I had to take inventory upon waking. It was my responsibility to make sure that those I loved were not removed from me in the stillness of the night while my father worked.

The reoccurring dream stopped when I saw that field, or what could have been that field.

It was one summer vacation in Italy as we drove from Florence to Siena to get a coveted prayer card for Seville Wilcox, my mother's dear friend. There it was through the window, the field I had seen in my dreams.

Excitedly, I told my parents about the dream and the field we had just passed, but they could not understand how that could be. I had never been there before, how could I have been dreaming about this place?

Later when we arrived in the Piazza di Campo after visiting S. Caterina, I sat in one of the pie shaped slices of the town square and surveyed the windows looking down on us as we ate gelato. I told my parents, I would have a home there one day and they laughed.

Only Gian was not laughing, he looked at me worried. We had been inseparable; Gian painfully shy, I had been his voice but now I was catching the wind and sailing, he would never leave the shore. The feeling that I was betraying him, abandoning him to his own devices made me feel guilty and ashamed of having faster dreams than he.

I was ten and he was twelve. We knew then what many never accept, that our home is laid in our souls; geography can start and end in our minds regardless of ever being there. Regardless of our life plans there is a travel voucher that comes with our destiny minus the legal disclosure and passenger bill of rights. What my parents ignored as a childish whimsy, my brother waited and hoped would not happen.

Eleven and a half years later on a rainy December morning, I eloped to marry my husband, Orazio in the providence of Siena.

No pomp and circumstance but a house in Siena nonetheless.

God put a few wrong people for us
to meet. Before we meet the right
one, so that when we finally do
meet that person, we should be
grateful for that gift.

~Unknown

Chapter 3: Rules

Dayton, Ohio, USA 1978

The rules are made to be broken. There are few who risk breaking the rules and thrive. Most rule breakers are just the few of us who blaze a trail; reveled as heroes but only long after they are gone. And there you have it, the meaning of life... Smack dab in the middle of the mirror staring back at you... you realize for a split second you are doing it again.

The heart tells you this is your chance. The inner voice tells you, not again. Between the consequences of the night before and the non-defining of a true goal, a true love, a true commitment, you realize that something is amiss. By all logical protocol you should listen to the inner voice; but something tells you it is different this time. "Your" heart, your essence tells you this is real and to hold on.

I continued to look in a mirror and talk to myself. I looked older than when I had run off to Canada. How long had it been?

ཨ The Other Side of Tuscany ཙ

Time ebbed in and out of my life, as if I changed the planets or their orbits; time just passes through me without logic or rules. Mrs. Grisseau had lobbied hard for me to stay in a special education class; "She's retarded," she had told my parents when I was in the first grade. She said I was "in-my-own-world", her only words that I did not mind. The others "retarded, retard, slow" stung like my father's hand on my chubby thighs.

Could she have been right? I could not focus and more times than not, I could not remember things. It was my literary musings written in a moment of distress that dislodged the morsels from my mind, some tasteful and others foreign objects that like a Christmas puzzle fresh from the box, I assembled the complete story.

Everyone was incredibly polite to me when I returned but no one dared ask me about my plans. I had taken a year off from the expensive fashion college in Atlanta to decide if I really wanted this, this dream that had been mine since I was a little girl. How simple it had been cutting up my father's socks and clothing all of my Barbies, and those of my playmates, in sleek little black dresses.

Marcella had said I had a knack; how could a five year old possibly know the rules of chic and class, accentuated by the perfect little black dress? I had not seen it for myself, my mother hated black having to wear it to grieve her dead mother most of her young life, now she wore rich vibrant color. When little girls asked for pink and lavender, I asked for black.

Mind you, these were my father's good socks some wool and cashmere blends. The ones he wore on

Sunday but more times than not, the ones he wore mix-matched; sometimes one shorter and one longer, sometimes one thin and one thick, but all times competing with the pant legs of his trousers to not be discovered by the parishioners at Immaculate Conception Catholic church.

The softness and simplicity of his socks made for a good, classic look and while my father was not making a fashion statement, I was. There was chatter of my talent and the possibilities that awaited me. There was also the uncertainty that came with trying to bridle a wild horse.

It just seemed that this dream was not possible without consequences, rules sautéed heavily with conundrum. London and most of Europe where I had set my sights was heavy with rules and steeped in tradition. I was a baker's daughter and a self-taught artist and seamstress, would I make it? Was it worth it, to go through all the expense of living in a foreign land, dealing with the A-types on a daily basis or settling down with "him" and maybe open a boutique in Toronto? At least in North America, I knew the ropes and had more tradition than most.

I certainly had the chops to break out on my own. I had organized fashion shows and fundraisers with just a year of college under my belt. I had learned from the best and generously kind staff at Neiman Marcus especially after the brutal chiding of my first interview with the Atlanta boutique T. Edwards. Neiman's had graciously hired me on my integrity; my talent was just a pleasant coincidence.

I was now designing windows for the Metropolitan and Paul Harris, sketching for the personal buyers, giving them options to sell their concepts through tantalizing images. Five or six well coordinated pieces a few great pairs of shoes maybe some boots and there you had it; 15 very different outfits in hand-sketched glory on the check-out counter. The sales people looked to me to help their clients spend more; the sketches showed clients how they were spending less. The proof was right there, in the sketches on the desk, and in the well-dressed mannequins in the window. Everyone was happy, why couldn't I be?

This could be a life… but where? Geography had always been my enemy. After my first trip to Europe, I had hoped one day there would be a bridge to connect the two countries.

I made and broke the rules. I was strong but damaged. I championed the underdog but could not stand up for myself. The defining moments of my life were stronger in the minds of others. Yet I had little recollection but for newspaper clippings my mother had saved. Had I "ruled out" my existence? Had pain suffocated the pleasure of remembering anything at all?

Vito was an amusing guy but clearly not the one even if he did share my grandfather's name. "Pop" as Grandpa was called, quite liked him, but who didn't? Vito Binetti was a smooth talker who could bring down civilizations with his smoke screen. He had charmed his way into his neighbor's bed yet it was she who was seen as promiscuous. Though he broke the rules, he expected me to follow them. His family adored me ever since I was a little girl vacationing in Canada but only the entrepreneurial Binettis understood and supported me when I wanted to break free from him.

"They" were not the majority; "they" specifically was "one", Domenic. While not a true relative, he was like the brother my father never had and had been a true achiever his whole life. Everyone admired and respected "Uncle Dom" as he was affectionately called. He had reached for dreams and achieved them- he wanted nothing more for a fellow *Paeseana* to do the same, especially if one were to be part of the gene pool that would be Binetti legacy.

My grandmother had died the summer before. There was no one really who needed me here, my sisters were entering adolescence so my parents could leave them home alone now. Gian was still reeling over Geri and some days, did not even seem like my brother. I wondered if that closeness we shared as children would ever return. He was losing focus, college was not for him. He was a "Rule Follower" and followed them into the bakery and out of his dreams.

As players danced in and out of our adult lives, the closeness that pushed one to better the other was lost. Some days I felt guilty for what he could have been. The magic I knew that taunted and tickled my fears also gave me the strength to always want more. I just assumed he had it too. Something kept the caterpillar from emerging from the dark and into the light. Later, sickness would give me a reason and peace from my questions. I felt that God had granted my brother solace by giving him an excuse.

I realized that the world had a set of rules and you were born either a follower or a breaker. My inner voice was a follower, my "heart" was a breaker and the essence of *"Malia"* was caught somewhere in between.

I heard the squeal of laughter coming from the closet and looked at the reflection of my sliding door to see, in the 3 inch crack, an eye, specifically the eye of my brother Gian. I reeled around and all the guilty feelings of abandoning him to his own plans evaporated and fueled rage like that of a locomotive. How long had he been hiding there watching me having a heart to heart conversation with my inner voice? I chased him out and slammed the door. I could hear him laughing and he descended the first short flight of stairs to the landing of the kitchen. Slip sliding in stocking feet, round the corner and down to the family room before retreating to his bedroom in the finished basement.

I was red-faced and flushed, the blood pulsing in my ears. That was it - easy - I was going. Gian just did me the biggest favor. I did not need this. I was not going to tell any of them until I was ready to leave. After all, I was good at secrets and most of them lived here. I could be whatever I wanted to be if I left the secrets behind.

Do you know where you're going to, do you know what life is bringing you…

The *Mahogany* song track played in the background and Diana Ross had just confirmed my fears. But I would make it. I would show them. Unlike the film, I would not fall into the love trap.

Success is nothing without someone to love.

How could she give it all away for a man? I wouldn't.

Like a switch, I turned off my North American connection and started my mental countdown to a country only visited in dreams: England.

Never say "Goodbye" when you
still want to try, never lose hope
unless you are sure of the results.

~Nac

Chapter 4: Leaving

Dayton, Ohio, USA 1977

Years ago, I arranged conference in Salt Lake City. One of the speakers was a young girl of about 15 whom we all knew had been battling a rare disease for years and was not expected to live to see her 16th birthday.

She opened her speech by saying, "I am so blessed because everything I taste is sweeter, every sunset and sunrise more beautiful, every person I meet - an instant friend. I have been fortunate to know that I need to regard each day as my last and because of that, I live in love and not fear; and I enjoy life to the fullest...

I only wish all of you could be as lucky as me!"

There are times that you feel closeness to your family in ways that are immeasurable and sacred. Then there are others. Sticky doorknobs, broken toasters and crumb trails turned into insurmountable obstacles that hinder conversations and well-planned meals. The age difference between my younger sisters, and Gian and I, left those early years filled with "insurmountable obstacles" for a social teenager.

In a self-imposed obligation to make up for having the only working mom on the street, I assumed her responsibilities. I saw my sisters as annoying obstacles that would weigh me and my dreams down if I did not leave. Linda and Sherry shared the physical likenesses to their personality counterparts. Linda, quiet with her red hair and slight build favored Gian. Sherry, daring with large inquisitive, brown eyes was like me. My younger sisters were, not only in how they looked but also in how they flowed through life, a rule follower and a rule breaker; a dreamer and a doctor, a student and a soccer player.

Rare were the moments in those early years that we would share the sorority that only women can share in the protection and nurturing of each other. They would write to me asking to take over my bedroom and belongings. On my visits home they would ask what I had brought them and where it came from. Some of it appreciated and some of it absurd and tossed into drawers. In their child-like minds, to understand that more was actually made up of things that were less and something was precious since it was purchased for them, in place of my next meal or cab fare was beyond a younger sister's comprehension.

One afternoon my mother broke the silence of my departure. My mother had only shared this with them because our relatives from Milan were visiting. We were arranging my Christmas holiday with them as to cut the expense of me traveling back and forth from London. Carla, my father's cousin's wife had helped build my wardrobe with the contest I had won at Paul Harris selling fur coats in August. I had garnered a $1000 shopping spree for my efforts and acting since I was very much against fur but it was the way out of Dayton drudgery and into my dreams. The bags all lay on my sister's bed. Linda annoyed at my disarray, had a new roommate with the arrival of our Italian guests. The real tension was the tightness about my departure and the amazement in not only my courage but that of my parents in letting me go.

I had never been to England and did not know a single soul. Since taking a year off from the Atlanta school, many of my former classmates had gone on to be the last graduating class in Lucerne and others still remained in Atlanta. Some had gone on to London only to find that the dollar had plummeted, that coupled with the irresistible offerings on Bond Street made that the parental subsidies insufficient. Despite wanting to continue, some had to return stateside.

I was convinced to find some sort of work despite not really being able to work as a US Citizen. I reassured my parents that between the scholarships and their help with tuition, I would be able to cover the rest of the expenses. Still, I had no idea *how,* except maybe a very rich Arab falling into my life. Later this would prove not to be such a far-fetched idea.

The three sisters sat on Linda's bed piled high with the selections of the shopping spree. The bordered, alpaca wool, circle skirt and silk blouses contrasted with the shorts sets made by Zia Maria and skinny, tan limbs of my little sisters.

"These clothes are *ugly*" said Sherry whose favorite color was purple. There was not one purple shred of cloth on the bed.

19

"Well, if you take blue and red you make purple. Just imagine these two blended..."

"They're still *ugly*" Sherry interrupted.

"Well, no one will care when I am famous- now will they? In fact, I will put together nice little *ugly* clothes for all you people back here in Dayton."

My sisters brought out the *best* in me.

My sister was solemn, pondering a world without purple clothes. I fell silent too. When would I see them again? They were smallish, but on the cusp of adolescence. I remembered how I became a *Donna Bambina (woman child)* overnight. Fortunately, for my sisters, they were unscathed from the horrors of early puberty and despite having to walk a full mile to school in kindergarten and first grade, had a relatively pleasant childhood.

That afternoon I realized that while I was willing them to be old enough to set me free, I would miss them and wished I could still protect and watch over them. I looked at the faces of my sisters; Linda's pinched in worry and pain, Sherry's brimming with wonder and tears. In that moment I wanted nothing more than to be strong and sure and defiant. I would not melt into a puddle of sobs; I was on the brink of greatness and they too needed to feel the power of that moment.

I got up and fiddled with the storm window, pulled up high to allow the breeze in. Our European guests did not appreciate air-conditioning and all the windows upstairs had been adjusted to accommodate them. I released the tab that held the thin, dull aluminum frame in place and wiggled it to set it free. The window, held now in front of me, I looked through the glass at my sisters. I imagined for a moment that they would be seeing me on a billboard. Balancing the frame on its edge I grabbed a permanent marker and with a flourish signed my moniker vertically across the glass.

Nac

"Better hang on to this. One day it is going to be worth something!"

I cheered wanting to lift the sadness.

Stunned, my sisters sat there. I handed the window over as if to say, "I'm off. Be happy for me"

Later, when my parents sold the house I wondered if the power of that moment had made the missing storm window sacred or if it was just another reason for my mother to be mad at me.

The sorority, the closeness that I felt that afternoon was colored in bittersweet

Goodbyes would return as the child sisters grew into women and visited me in Tuscany and later in Carolina.

I wonder now, if the moments were so precious because of their economy or if they were a divine reward for those that made time for each other? Just like the dying girl and a precious, single day or like the song we carry in our hearts for those we will always love?

She not only survived; she became.

~Teri Saint Cloud, Bone Sign Arts

Chapter 5: The Cost of Protection

Impruneta, Tuscany, Italy 1980

I had interviewed with Gandolfo Gandolfi the
spring I was at the house of Pucci. I had been
unhappy in haute couture and all the political
underpinnings that made fashion. It was not about
sketching but about rules that I did not want to play
by.

It seemed like a reasonable alternative at the time: I
would still design only it would be prêt a porter
instead of couture, I could stay in Italy just as a
conservative daughter of Gandolfo and not a free
spirited jet-setter. Lastly, I could figure out what I
wanted to do without pressure. If I went back to
Dayton, the safety net a family provides while
snatching ambition, might just capture me.

I reluctantly contacted the Gandolfi family to come
and pick me up from my Florentine apartment. It
was a compromise.

I had been in Florence about a month after a
confusing and tumultuous few weeks in Bari at the
sea. How could my mother's relatives be so dear to
her heart? They were barbaric and crude, full of
money without principle or respect. Their very
existence, a magazine page: all superficial gloss

with the depth of the thinness of the page it was printed on.

The men of the Bari brood, posing as well - meaning "cousins" had ushered me into Italian domestic hell through a salmagundi of lies, infidelity and rape. Someone had stolen the money I had set aside for the rest of my studies and rent before starting my new job in Florence. Even if I did not want to participate in their game, they paid for everything that was needed. I had come this far, I could not go back and this would have to do.

While the control they had over me was real, my apparent complacency to accept the fate was not. By obliging, it would end sooner. In my mind it was never me and in an odd sort of way I felt I was in control. I would float away just as I had as a young girl, sometimes I would hum. It unnerved them to see that I regarded their sex as a sport or exercise. There was no disgust, no resistance it was just an act and I could turn off any emotion and get up as if nothing ever happened. Why didn't I tell Lana, my mother's cousin or her husband?

When my husband would describe me later to his lover, he said I was a beauty without a soul: *Bella Sensa Anima.* I am sure this made many regard me as a monster of sorts when in reality it was merely a tactic for survival, when you live hiding the sins of others.

Men have a history of taking from women without remorse, a birthright to having a meat dagger between their legs. I regarded my body not as a temple but as wardrobe. Rape requires a change of wardrobe, a change of scenery. I was good at that, careful to keep my soul untouchable.

The words of my mother still fresh from our recent visit to Florence, betraying her maternal protection of me as barter for a job to be proud of. My mother in her naïveté had no idea what she was asking and had no idea what I had already been through.

Rape is a double-edged sword to those that survive it. In protecting one's self we find a strength that is without a soul, mercenary in its survival, explicit in thriving in a cast of characters. An expert secrecy allows the roles not to overlap. If I could tell my mother, it would show the true colors of her hometown; the thievery and deceit that later would be the laying down of these families and their wealth.

I seemed to have situations imploding all around me and while I watched as if from a distance, I was in the midst of it. Beppe di Bari had come to the Ionic Riviera one day to meet me pushed from Gandolfo's urgings while I was in Bari. Gandolfo had already imagined us the perfect match. Beppe a single family friend was their top producer and his family was ingrained in the upper crust of the south where a woman will starve herself to afford the right dress. Gandolfo had described me as a young, catalyst of a designer who seemed to attract attention and publicity without trying, was coming to work for him and he had wanted us to meet at all costs. This was what the Hofel label needed to be revitalized and made pristine he suggested.

Beppe di Bari was expecting to find an unattractive heavy-set Italo-Americana. Later he reported to Gandolfo, instead he found a heavier version of Carolina di Monaco with an incredible mouth, willing lips and mischievous eyes that sparkled as if the very fire within was reflected in them. Her bottom full and round with a waist so unnaturally small that it gave her an irresistible feminine silhouette. Her hair seemed immeasurable that one could be lost in it for hours, raven with red lights when the sun kissed it, light and dancing when teased by the wind.

I could see that he was so taken by my appearance as he sheepishly concealed his pleasure with his wicker basket that he had brought, brimming with white wine and Foccaccia, sun-dried tomatoes, figs, almonds and olives. I had noticed but hoped no one else did. I knew I needed all the allies I could get, my having Beppe also in my "grasp" was one more favor I could call. Whatever it would take…

Despite being Italian and despite being adventurous in London, nothing prepared me for the double standards and primitive interactions of courtship and family. I had lived on my own four years, had seen and done things that made me blush just thinking of writing them. Remembering them now, or more accurately forgetting them, I think of my own daughters and say a secret prayer that they never experience what I have.

Holy Father, keep their girlfriends safe too, so they will never have to listen to cracked voices, the ones that choke back tears, and wonder if they can ever trust again. Protect them. My blood is on your altar.

Driven by the forces of love, the
fragments of the world seek each
other so that the world may come
into being. Love alone is capable of
uniting living beings in such a way
as to complete and fulfill them, for
it alone takes them and joins them
by what is deepest in themselves.

~*Pierre Teilhard de Chardin*

Chapter 6: Behind Gates

Impruneta, Tuscany, Italy 1981

Gandolfo's daughters had allowed me a few moments of freedom that morning as I was not one to shop. They had told me that I could wait at the bar after my hair was done and they would come within a few hours. I had waited before and I knew that "a few hours" in Italian- shopping- time- could be an entire day. I had opted for a *"miscommunication"* and had decided that when I was through, I would walk the 2 kilometers home.

Earlier my eyes welled with tears as the Nora worked on my hair. The stylist's scissors skillfully clipped, even when I could not see any hair between her fingers. It was almost as if the blades were teasing me and my thinning hair. I tried not to let the stylist see my tears; more rumors would ensue if the culling tears were to roll down my cheeks. I really did not need any more grief from gossip. I was sad to cut my hair but I would be even unhappy if Ophelia, my *Hofel* boss heard any rumors, blaming her for my sadness. My hair had started to fall out from the stress. Some of the workers had said Ophelia had pulled my hair out when she was angry and that was the reason it was missing in clumps.

I always had long hair except when there was a life changing event in my life: the birth of a little sister, the cancer of a brother, the death of a friend. Once my brother and I had conspired to "see" what was inside my raven rope-like plaits. My hair was as stubborn and unpredictable as I was - sometimes curling without warning or tangling with a sudden burst of wind. So it was for this reason my mother, Annabelle kept the unruly locks fastened in long, thick braids. To my older sibling, Gian, the braids intrigued him as if they were appendages of sorts. So one day, he decided to cut one of my plaits and look inside. He was much too young to think of the consequences, or to think of what to do with the unfortunate braid.

The incident was late one summer night when I was three or four. My father Rinaldo, returning from one of his pastry jobs, noticed the braid. He pulled the white Chevy station wagon that smelled of glazed donuts and noticed what appeared to be a dead animal into the driveway. There was something odd about the beast, but not wanting to spoil his dinner with a closer examination, he kicked the presumed carcass aside and went inside. He kissed my mother lightly on the cheek and asked what was for dinner while our small family assembled at the Formica table.

Uncle Dan was the first to sit down and reaching down grabbed me at the waist and swung me into a mint green high chair that was too small. The table only had four chairs and despite the lack of comfort,

I was the youngest and therefore sat in the high chair without the tray. Every time my mother suggested that Gian sit in the high chair and let me sit in his chair, Gian would wail desperately. Our mother would plead,

"Pleeez Gianni, yoor sister is a butter ball and you more skinny."

Gianni was never convinced; and I was stuffed into the high chair, silent, because it seemed otherwise I would miss my meal and never have a real chair. In my daydreams, I sat on a throne made of royal icing, satin and lace, dotted with tiny, silver sugar balls like the tiny crib Papa had made for me when I was born.

CS SO

In England, my hair had been my strength, my glory. My raven mane could be cropped in the shows for Wembley in September, and then was ready for weaving and pruning again in May; such was the health and thickness of it.

"You have amazing, amazing hair," the Revlon representative had said as he interviewed me to represent them at the next show.

"Well, If you use me and my hair that will be at least 100 quid" I remarked.

I was pushing; the others were getting 25 British Pound Sterling a day, a quarter of what I was asking. I had caught a glimpse of my reflection in the tube window as I rode out to the interview. I could see that I was stunning. My skin was white and kissed with freckles. My hair as dark as the

night and oriental as silk, and my eyes pools of chocolate that turned green with tears. I could be Irish or Italian or a mix of sorts. Make-up further confused my origin and I enjoyed the mystery not tying me to one particular land. It was almost as if freedom had lifted a veil of insecurity and provinciality and replaced it with allure.

"The show is only four days long what makes you so special?" He had inquired.

"Well, I can converse in four languages...and cuss in about 25 if they fuck-up my hair! You won't be disappointed."

And with that, I threw back my head accentuating just how beautiful and luxurious my hair really was. Competition was fierce and while it was not my true nature to be so brash in my self-promotion, it was survival so I played the part. The Revlon director in charge of putting together the Revlon Angels; a brunette, a blond and a redhead, wanted to make sure he did not lose this trans-cultural look, so he agreed on the price, not really sure if I was joking.

᭍᭠

My long hair was now short. As I walked and mourned my hair I heard an unfamiliar horn of a Mercedes behind me. It was Orazio, who I had met only briefly at a dinner for the Grape Festival, offering me a lift.

Though we had seen each other almost on a daily basis working at the *Santa Maria's* float for the pageant, this would be the first time we had actually spoken. It really hit me sitting close in the car how much I was attracted to him, how he was soft spoken and gentle, unlike the man I had seen shouting at the workers working on-site. His curling chestnut hair matched his long lashes. He had thick jet-black brows framing kind eyes that held a similarity to the markings of his German shepherd "Yago". He reminded me of *"Little Joe"* from *Bonanza*[1] in his looks and demeanor. I could see he was attracted to me by his nervousness, when he reached across to help me with the seat, I could see that he was slightly shaking.

Once he and his friends met me, they obsessed with *my oddities* traits that made me different and rare in their circles. The bags of apples I ate in horse-like fashion. The molding and braiding of my hair like pieces of pastry when I was not at ease. And the constant smile on my face even when people were not particularly nice to me. Of most concern, was that I was American, so how I had come, I would surely leave, and no one found any reason to get to know me better.

It was when I did not leave and the toils of my work situation had started to wear on my health that Orazio began to get concerned and interested in my welfare. I was becoming dangerously thin every time he saw me and it seemed of no one's concerns. He had asked his sister Anna, who was one of Gandolfo's daughters sister's in law to pick me up and bring me to dinner whenever she could. He had wanted to help me, to make sure I was fed but mostly, despite being engaged he wanted to get to know me better.

---

[1] Played by a young Michael Landon, the popular western aired in the 1960s and was re-run all over the world for many years.

He had been told that winter when I left to go back to the states that I had a crush on him but knowing my plans, I did not want to upset what seemed like a comfortable situation for him. Besides, I quite liked his fiancée, Alicia. Of all the females that frequented the *Casina*, the tiny chapel restored as Orazio and Alessandro's bachelor Pad, she was the only one who tried to communicate with me. She was kind and perceptive and when she sat next to me, we would shock each other; such was the electricity between us. When she noticed Orazio admiring my backside she asked me about my private life.

"Live in Italy? Are you crazy? I could never go back in time I must go forward. I love it here but it is so hard to live in this country after living in America. Besides, I'm engaged." I had been engaged to Vito before leaving for London and while I never really officially broke off the engagement, he was sleeping with his neighbor and I was keeping peace by not making a big deal. "La faccia", (the face) was important to Italians everywhere whether they lived in Canada or Dayton, London or Florence. I had mastered "the face"; I knew how to keep everyone happy.

I saw Alicia had smiled, that was all she needed, the confirmation that I was leaving and never coming back.

You may never know the results of
your actions but if you do nothing
there will be no results.

~Mahatma Gandhi

Chapter 7: Spoils of Gucci

Florence, Tuscany, Italy 1982

There are so many gauges and parts to a life in
constant reinvention, that at one time while
conducting *un stage* at Gucci, the Signorina
Ballerina commented,

"We find it hard to believe that someone of your
age has had the opportunity to have done all these
things"

It was true at twenty-two I had a wealth of
experience: I had worked at the bakery since I was
tall enough to see over the counter and what's more,
had a long list of community service. What the
Signorina did not understand was the American
practice of service which made my already
extensive resume, seem just impossible to be real.
Why would anyone, especially a young person who
could be in discothèques and cinemas enjoying
themselves "play" with special children or read to
the elderly? In all fairness, the Signorina probably
did not know where Dayton, Ohio was; and that it
was not exactly a Mecca for night life and cultural
happenings.

ℰ The Other Side of Tuscany ℭ

What I could not get past was that she was calling me a liar. A full resume of varied experiences had to be a bold-faced falsehood, especially to an old spinster married to the house of Gucci.

Why did I not stand up for myself?

Getting the job at Gucci may have been the lynchpin of me being, and me not being, the misfit in my Tuscan life. Those things were true. The problem was that in Italy most young people either worked or studied, if they did community service it was usually in lieu of mandatory military service. What could have easily been dismissed as a cultural difference was dismissed as if I were just the Forrest Gump of fashion chatting up Signorina Ballerina over a box of chocolates.

So there I sat, in a room seething with jealousy and flamboyance, fielding with grace the insults to my bakery background, the Maria Joseph Home and Special Olympics. I was fresh; I was innocent to the power play. I did not realize then that what we give and do in our lives is what makes us; no one can or should take that away. I had talent that had not been influenced by the industry, yet rather than show the Chutzpah that had gotten me to Europe in the first place, I cowered, fearing any minute I would hear my father's voice asking about a cake I forgot to do.

I lowered my head not in shame but resignation. Would I ever be understood? Would there be a place for kindness and doing without motive? Not here.

If anything, I can thank the dear Signorina for giving me what would be a life-long commitment: making prerequisite for any company I would work

33

for, a plan for social responsibility and marketing that directly tied to a good greater than the company or its products. Today it is commonplace but in the 1980s it was unusual and odd to be a do-gooder when not of church or aristocratic blood.

I had come to the Gucci presentation after my initial interview with Mr. Fitzpatrick, anxious and happy with possibilities, dancing. Anna, Orazio's sister had driven me in an aqua blue *Cinquecento* (Fiat 500) and waited outside. "In Bocca al Lupo" she had wished me good luck with the Tuscan version of *Break a Leg,* and my eyes grew wide at someone telling me to jump in the wolf's mouth. Later she would explain the expression and the response, "Che Creppi" *May he (the wolf) die.*

I had felt among peers when I first arrived at the Gucci Lab. As the testing went on, only to see that they were like everyone else, judging me in black and white, turning virtues into flaws, shunning me as a liar; as if I were a stray cat that had wandered into Gucci's door after being fed by one of my own, Mr. Fitzpatrick, the American general director.

I lived in constant fear. I knew it would kill me; it made me wish I were dead some days just to have some peace. It was not something I could pinpoint, it was like I was always doing something wrong but I did not know what right was. I felt like a stray cat at Gandolfi's and later, with my husband's family and still later, in his house. I felt I never knew the rules and therefore, broke them. Yet, I could not leave-my parents had been steadfast that I marry before returning to Italy or I was lost to them. I knew what I could accomplish if I could look past the nagging feeling of inadequacy-but some days I just could not. Some days even though courage was a much better option, I just could not get past it, the debilitating terror that was knotted about me; made me feel like the walking dead. I had the same feelings growing up after my cousin told me everyone would die one day. I was small, three or four, but that simple obvious statement to an unsuspecting child left me with a dull pang of fear that would accompany me the greater part of my childhood.

From the possibilities at Gucci, to the lack there of, at Gandolfi. How different would my life have been, had I not felt so vulnerable working under a Machiavellian CEO and her geriatric husband? He had wanted to circumvent his daughters in giving me his fashion empire; one that he had started and they had no interest in continuing.

He believed in me and the more he did, the more they discredited him and our work together. I lived in constant fear and alertness; knowing the slightest inattention would bring the walls around me crumbling down and a humiliating return to the United States to a community that expected so much more from me.

Anna insisted, "Just call him, tell him, you are here and not in Fagnigola, what is the big deal?"

The big deal was that Gandolfo did not like her brother and had already picked Beppe for me to marry. Orazio was an unwelcome distraction. Gandolfo gave generously only because he had a plan for its repayment, and that schedule did not include my falling in love with Orazio. He was good to me in the privacy of our conversations, but even then, I was fearful. I remember how he touched me that April afternoon when we tried on

35

linen suits before deciding on a bright yellow linen one.

"Take it, it is a gift. Go ahead."

This was before I understood how very important it was to enable the generosity of those who were able to give. I unfortunately had always been just able to get by, I had friends who would give gifts on a whim, but I had never had this luxury. The display of kindness left me feeling obligated and inadequate; a feeling that I would not lose until later in life, one that sometimes prevented me from keeping the lines of love open because I could not reciprocate.

"Beppe" Giuseppe Andria was from Bari, a blue blooded family like Gandolfo Gandolfi's a bit more pomp and less circumstance but *Noble* nonetheless. He was the son, of those holding the most profitable region for the design house and he, in his own right, the prince of ready- to - wear in the south. He not only sold each line in great numbers he built it stealing snippets of creativity from the masters and adding the baroque quality needed to appeal to the South. Beppe single-handedly had made the House of Hofel profitable when the designs started to get stale. Gandolfo was quick to acknowledge this, yet his wife grudgingly would accept his inspirations or those of anyone else for that matter, only when the proof was in the numbers. Ophelia was a severe and bitter woman, who patronized me and when she could not blame me for my shortcomings, she took joy in insulting my mother for them.

What had my mother done to deserve this except come from Southern Italy?

Had she heard what my mother had said to me when we met with her husband, Gandolfo last August?

Everything that irritates us about
others can lead us to an
understanding of ourselves.

~Carl Jung

Chapter 8: Customs Cancer

Milan, Lombardia, Italy 1980

That Christmas, Gandolfo's daughters and Anna,
excitedly prepared to accompany me to the States. I
was going to treat them to the pre-Christmas glitter
of my home town as we would say good-bye and I
would remain in the states. It was to be a peaceful
time, put behind the jealousy and allow for me to
return some of the kinder moments we had shared
in their country but hosting them in mine.

What they did not know is that I was carrying cash
for Gandolfo's sister, Marcella, who was in Dayton
and getting Cancer treatments that were of
exorbitant cost. At the time, there were cash
restrictions of only £250.000 ($200.00) that could
leave the country per trip. I was carrying 50 times
the legal amount for Italy. Gandolfo trusted me and
knew I would get the money to his sister, as I had
before on other trips. I could talk my way out of the
declaration in NYC with this personal tragedy. The
fear the word Cancer struck, in those early days,
made all infractions forgivable. This time, it was
important to do without the knowledge of his wife
and daughters. Gandolfo dearly loved his younger
sister and had often broken the rules to send her
money. He could not risk any more infractions with

the financial police. His wife had been very angry with him the last time as she could not understand the high price of medicine and suspected there was some degree of frivolity involved.

At the airport, the Malpensa officers were thorough. I expected to be stopped by the young officer, I always was. Though, I did not expect them to un-wrap the terracotta bakers that were to be Christmas presents. In the bell shaped, hollow figures I had stuffed rolls of hundred dollar bills. I turned to Anna to tell her when I realized I was going to be detained. I wanted her to know that it wasn't my money and if something should happen she had to get it to Marcella and not say anything to the girls. Confused, she nodded, but when the Captain was called and the daughters looked through the glass partition and saw the wads on money being unrolled on the security counter, her concern was obvious worry. After all, I had come from nowhere highly recommended with an entourage of famous acquaintances, photographers and well-known playboys but no real proof of who I was except for my talent.

"Well, well two and a half years without working in Europe, Little Lady. It looks like she has a nice, little side business going on." The Captain finished his sermon to his men and they laughed.

The smell of wool uniforms pregnant with sweat and stale cologne reminded me that they were excited to have "a catch". I reminded them I needed a woman and someone from the Embassy before any more clothes were coming off. Then it came to me – I had a cousin who worked at the Malpensa airport. In fact, if I counted my cousin Norina's husband, I had two.

In Italy, there is power in who you know and even more in family. While I was taken to a small cubicle and the memories of being in a den of hungry men stirred my fears, I remembered my purpose and that the money was neither mine nor theirs for the taking. I found courage in my disgust for these men and their unsaid importance.

"Please call my cousin, Giam Piero Torresan."

"Giam Piero is your cousin?"

They were confused; I had an American Passport that clearly stated my birthplace in Dayton, Ohio. My cousin while not senior at the airport had several friends who were and he was influential, well-respected and liked. Giam Piero arrived and was not amused to see me in the small room filled with the chaos the aftermath "a search" brings: suitcases dumped, shoes removed, gloves ready and money being counted and rearranged in piles.

"Ma che cazzo fate!?!"alarmed to see me half-dressed and all the piles of money. Fearing that I may have something to say just to him, he switched to English.

"It's not what you think…" I started and so did the tears.

As he cleaned my mascara with his handkerchief, it was obvious to the men that I was a lot younger than I appeared. They were saddened and ashamed, as my cousin translated the tale of Gandolfo's sister and how I was risking breaking the law to save her life, even if it would be for just one more Christmas.

The Other Side of Tuscany

While the officers allowed me to compose myself before returning to the gate and the money to hiding, they reminded me that I would be on my own at JFK in New York. That did not frighten me half as much as being on the long flight with the daughters and their nasty accusations. As we landed in New York, news that John Lennon had been gunned down in front of his apartment was on the wire, December 8th 1980. The hysteria of his passing was enough to erase the security episode and pass on to more important topics- like *Shopping.*

As fate would have it, not long after the girls returned home from their US holiday, I received a call from their father, Gandolfo. Hofel's lead designer was ill and they needed me to finish the collection. Would I come? They would give me whatever was possible if I said "yes."

I knew what I wanted but he was the only thing that they could not and would not want to.

"The curtain would come down." Gandolfo had said.

Orazio would be the reason Gandolfo would close his heart to me the rest of my days in Italy and the rest of his days on this earth.

Was this an omen, or the curse of the curtain that followed me through my childhood?

The color of my soul is iron-grey
and sad bats wheel about the
steeple of my dreams.

~Achille-Claude Debussy

Chapter 9: The Iron Curtain

Impruneta, Tuscany, Italy 1981

When I was a little girl, the grown-ups talked about an iron curtain. I never really knew where this particular curtain was but those on "the other side" were bad people and those that were on "this side" were good. Somewhere between the curtain's "being" and "not being", there were people and things caught on sides where they did not belong.

Before I eventually moved to Tuscany permanently and forgot the metal drapery of my childhood, I would often wake from dreams, shaken from the screams of the souls who were caught. Though waking would quell the dream, the angst that filled my chest from the pain would not subside. I felt their sense of a dangerous "not belonging', I felt their entrapment but probably most important, I felt I was to help them find their way. Some nights I did not want to go to bed. I hated the dreams that taunted me. I hated the impotence of not being able to help. Though I held out my hand, no one could reach it.

I often wondered why no one had ever tried to unravel the mesh that made the curtain - look for an area that was compromised; stick a finger through a weathered, sun-bleached pleat. In all the years I heard mention of that "curtain" it was never unraveled or compromised. Those who were caught went about their days making the best of their lot. The generations and generations who followed soon forgot that there was a better place - no one talked of it. What they had, even if it was not good, was accepted.

How could I survive the rest of my days wondering what could or could not have been with Orazio?

The Gandolfi were more and more difficult to work for and live with. Now that I had returned I had no choice but to comply with their rules; the rules which included always being accompanied since I was younger than Gandolfo's daughters and kidnapping was prevalent those days. They thought best to make sure I was never left alone. They had felt with my good nature, I could easily trust the wrong person or be taken by mistake instead of one of the wealthy daughters.

Anna had proved a valuable ally. Often she would be my chaperone taking me to dinners where she knew I would see Orazio or asking him to accompany me on errands that Gandolfo had sent me to do with her.

Ophelia was outraged each time she felt I was seeing Orazio or anyone outside of the strict boundaries they had set. Of all the youth who had come calling and hoping to entertain me, they had made an exception for Marco, a young journalist who was injured and confined to a wheel chair. They had reported to my parents that Spring that I was dead to them, only because one afternoon I had been late in coming back from the Vallenbrosa. I had been with Anna, their daughter and the respective husbands yet someone had snitched under the pressure of interrogation and mentioned that Orazio was also there.

Our tardiness, which would become a fate-laced pattern, accompanied us in good fortune and in moments like these. It was not our fault, the errand we left for also included a stop to pick up blades from the artisan who fixed the massive ribbon-like blades from the sawmill. He had left for a funeral that afternoon and not yet returned. Not that we did not make good use of our "waiting time" making love in a secluded grove before the climb upward to the mountain resort of Vallombrosa.

I still shiver at the thought of risking being one of the *Mostro di Firenze's* casualties in our carnal, very public affection those early years. I say a hushed and desperate prayer every time I think of the heinous crimes of the notorious "Guardone" Pietro Pacciani, said Monster of Florence. Ironically, in my last years in Tuscany, he would kill his final victims in the woods of our Scopeti home, confirming my fears, that danger is always closer than you think.

Life is not the way it's supposed to
be. It's the way it is. The way you
cope with it is what makes the
difference.

~Virginia Satir

Chapter 10: Straddling the Chasm

Impruneta, Tuscany, Italy 1982

Marriage is a journey not a set destination. I think
young brides or at least; the isolated ones like me,
have only films and mothers to gauge this journey.
The only friends I knew that were married had
needed to get married to excuse their growing
abdomens. My parents were among the few parents
who believed in the vow- "'til death do us part."
And those vows scared the hell out of me.

People were getting divorced and people were not
getting married at all. Before I left the states, even
provincial, behind-the-times Dayton, Ohio had
"swingers." I was straddling a chasm I had not
expected. I had wanted to get married only after I
had lived my life. I was a wild one, yet I believed in
marriage, for what my parents had believed:
through richer and poorer, in sickness and in health.
I wanted someone to share stories with in my old
age.

My path was decided when I decided to live in a
foreign country, and that did not include the jet
setting single years I had envisioned. There is a
journey within all of us, the path is not always clear,

but a "Foglio di Via"[1] can make decisions very quickly for you, if you are on the fence. While not always the view true to our expectations or life plans. What is always true is that the journey is there and that plans are just rules that we impose on a perfectly happy life.

When I first met Orazio, I made a pact with myself that this would be the best part of my journey on earth. I vowed each day would be filled with wonder and new things, and no matter how mundane the task, I would make it amusing. I remember the first 365 days of our life together he did not eat the same thing twice unless he requested it. I felt I needed to prove that, yes, Americans can cook even if it meant hours of combing kitchen diaries of the great masters.

I may have initiated this pact, because I was scared of a normal life. I had not imagined a married life, yet Orazio would sit down at the large oak table that he had made and point to the head of the table. When I asked if something was missing, he would then point and say,

"A little one right here."

That scared me. I was not even sure I could have children. I would imagine all that I had been through, with the exception of some cutting and scraping, had left me all but barren. I feared that had damned me and would make him leave me when he found out that I could not bear him children. Then there was that inner voice, "it will never last." His

---

[1] Expulsion papers when one has overstayed the tourist visa and has basically been caught in infraction. They are delivered with a date to leave the country my date was December 9th 1981.

fiancée had been all too clear in her curse to us when he told her that he was leaving her for me.

There was the Italian wives' adage that there were two types of women: the ones men married and the ones men loved. The lovers were the ones that did the things wives shouldn't do. The marrying types were for the home and bearing children. These fine women were the ones who cooked and cleaned and wore the finest clothes and jewelry on Sunday, and "Le Corne[2]" Monday through Saturday.

I was confused by these rules. I was caught on the wrong side of the curtain and the ocean to make sense of it. Even the most obvious was oblivious to me, 'Le Corne' or the horns. In my naïveté, I assumed when someone was wearing the horns, they were the devilish one, the one being mischievous and in explicit sins: the one committing adultery. Imagine my surprise to find it to be the direct opposite. If you had horns on your head, your husband or wife was cheating on you, and everyone knew. Much like wearing a dunce cap, everyone could see these magnificent horns on your head.

"Se Orazio se...." "If Orazio finds horns on his head, he will scratch them," my boss at Giomar, a manufacturer for Paolo Gucci had mused once since Orazio almost never wanted to go anywhere with me.

---

[2]Your husband is cheating on you. The crown jewel of insults, "le corne" also implies that the person is being cheated upon. Usually applied during heated arguments in the middle of the road, after one's garage exit is blocked or crazy driving has taken place.

My husband, especially during my designing years, allowed envious friends and relatives to stir his jealousy. He would imagine large winding horns from his head, such were the implied affairs, such were the flirtatious insinuations. It did not help that my lack of understanding left me nodding to accusations by jealous wives, because I would address everyone informally with "tu" instead of "lei".

"When did you ever eat together!?!" Eyes opened wide, in a pitch high and loud, they would announce in what never failed to be a very public place, accompanied by menacing hand gestures.

"Si," I would reply, not understanding anything but "eat" and "together" thinking innocently that the nice strangers just met at the market or shops wanted to invite us to "eat together."

Mom always said I never knew a stranger…

Still in another instance as a new wife, I allowed my husband and his single friend Massimo, to corral about town warning them not to come home with horns on. Good natured, Massimo had said,

"Hmm, is Nancy French? I thought she was American."

While my husband laughed, later when he returned he tried to explain never to make those proclamations again, especially not to someone known to be a rumor mill about town.

I truly meant no harm in the beginning, but lack of understanding was my accomplice. As I grew to interpret colloquialisms and the bi-forked lashes, I

❧ The Other Side of Tuscany ❧

took pride in perfecting innocence to the height of insult, clever and cunning; I would circulate their lies, to keep the rumor mill churning and neighbors fighting. It delighted me to have such importance in the day to day storytelling, that was, until, the little quips intended for quarrels and learning moments in the danger of gossip, backfired like the beast rising from Dr. Frankenstein's lab.

Years after leaving Tuscany simple stories had grown into loquacious lies. Never did I think that monsters grew even without the creators feeding. Now I regret the childishness of getting even, but I have more than paid the price.

Through the hardest journey we
need take but one step at a time but
we must keep stepping despite the
difficulties.

~Chinese Proverb

Chapter 11: Marriage

Mezzano, Tuscany, Italy 1984

Italian love stories are much like that idyllic, poppy polka-dotted countryside into which, amidst spring flowers and promise, an iron curtain is dropped. There is a foreign film quality to riding a motor bike around windy hills dotted with stucco villas and terracotta roofs with a long loaf of crusty bread under your arm, while balancing a straw-covered flask between your legs. Coupled with the intoxicating anticipation of a light lunch in a secluded olive grove and making love in the open area without getting caught or photographed by "guardoni" (Peeping Toms).

This phase of innocence and picnics, passes on to a formal marriage or in our case a "Foglio di Via" (expulsion papers) where a decision must be made to formalize the union or leave the country. We opted for marriage and while this was what we ultimately wanted, we wanted it on our terms not on immigration's.

I confided in Rina, Orazio's mother, that once the announcement[1] was posted if no one disputed our union, we would be married on December 19th a week before Christmas.

It had been four months since I had returned to Tuscany without my family's blessing. Orazio had told my father that summer when he had come for me that he did not believe in getting married for decorum and if my father was worried about him providing for me, he was wrong. If it got down to the wire, Orazio had told my father, he could write a bigger check.

My husband was proud like that. Once when he could not come to agreement with a driver as to who should back down the narrow street of the Scopeti per Montbuoni - a medieval road designed for horses without possibilities for two cars, my husband simply stopped the car and instructed us (me and the children) to walk home. In doing so, he blocked the road for everyone else and proved his point that he was not compromising and that he also lived closer to his destination than the unfortunate driver that wanted to pass.

For examples like this, he was respected as well as hated, not just by those who did not know him, but also by his family.

Despite these oddities, I was terribly in love with my husband as he was with me, despite my stubbornness and irrationality. Sister Bernadette had compared me to *Zelda* when I was in the sixth

---

[1] In Italy, the civil union of two people was posted for three weeks before a civil ceremony was preformed. In that way, if one was married or knew of another union that would conflict there was plenty of time for the marriage to be stopped.

grade-was it compliment or intuition? I wondered if she had seen a streak of insanity that reminded her of Fitzgerald's wife or if she imagined that innate elegance was a legacy passed through creative minds. Was our love a mere gauntlet we threw down to defy fate? Or was it the bravura of two people proving the pundits wrong even if love was no guarantee.

A forced marriage, as he would later tell me was not how he envisioned spending his life with someone. Though he loved me, he was waiting for the other stiletto to fall, that day I would harness the wind and leave. He had seen this with so many "mixed marriages" and my own history confirmed that when I could not change things to my liking, I changed venue. Further complicating our story was the constant stream of competition that seemed untiring to undermine our union.

My husband was extremely jealous. Italian men have no tact when appraising beautiful women. They can go as far as rubbing up against your backside so that you can "feel" their appreciation. This was one source of our arguments.

Another sore spot was his family, since he did not have a father; he felt a responsibility to take care of his mother, sister and her husband. Anna, his sister had confided that she had used the dowry his mother set aside for Orazio and his wife. One day she confessed when I asked for the towels we desperately needed as I was not permitted to purchase any since I had them in my dowry.

"Well of course I used the things set aside for my brother. No one ever expected him to get married… then you came along."

I felt cheated, like I was not good enough to have what everyone else marrying into the family received and the signing of the prenuptial dividing our properties only confirmed my sentiments and their mistrust.

Our arguments were ignited not of things that stemmed from us but from others; my voice fueling the discussion with concerns that I would never have anything to call my own.

Rina, my mother –in- law was my ally; she understood my feelings, as well as, understanding the entrapment of unconditional love. Before Alzheimer's' would rob us of our conversations, she would tell me how much our love story reminded her of the struggles she and Orazio's father shared. A family of farmers turned entrepreneurs; they were communists. She reminded me that in the family this meant, what was "yours was mine and what was mine was mine."

She would warn me, "Take care to have something for you and your children or you will be missing the earth from beneath your feet."

I thought these warnings were a result of bitterness having lost her husband and having to work alongside her brothers-in-law to have her "piece of earth". She worked just as hard as the men, if not harder. I mimicked her despite the warning.

Unfortunately, for a young designer who was street smart, I had been left "white road naïve." I had worked in the fashion industry and retired after the birth of my twins Benji and Gemma but never dreamed the people that I thought friends would turn on me once I was out of earshot or had left the country. Worse, I never expected them to crawl into my bed.

Granted, I had always been different, did not have many "girlfriends" and the fact, that most of my friends were men and my acquaintances flamboyant, artistic and unusual had always fueled controversy. The fact I did not change or make an attempt at conformity after I married, nor openly cared, made me untouchable and rare.

Rina was right. As sickness took her mind, her family squabbled over her land and her possessions. The closeness I knew in my own family left me unprepared to deal with a "foreign family feud". Warfare, whatever the degree, needs "like minds" or you are merely a cat, strutting into a dog fight. My solution was to leave and remove the ones I love, to a land for which no one could lay claim.

My husband Orazio, in his own way, dealt with conflict much the same way. He moved me to a country house where I spent 5 years of our life starting our family at a distance to his birthplace and immediate family. Still, the small town, Strada in Chianti at the foot of the hill, was intrigued by "this woman" who received so much mail even a telegram from Dino De Laurentis once and foreign visitors.

I rarely was seen with my husband due to his hours and dislike of espresso. Instead, I was seen more often with his partner, Alessandro or other associates of his business. This further complicated the small town chatter.

ಬ The Other Side of Tuscany ಣ

I freelanced and dreamed and wrote and sculpted in the Imprunetean Terracotta while raising our children. Though I was devoted, I could not possibly be a "good" mother since I had so many interests and "real mothers" did not.

I did not queue up to get veal brains on Thursday or fresh ricotta on Tuesday. My children ate eggs from the supermarket or shop and not from the farmer. Horrible-American-Stranger- Mother I was, I even let my children play in the rain and jump in puddles, wear cotton undershirts instead of wool and I washed my hair as soon as I gave birth.

The Isolation of the house above the small blue collar town was refreshing from the vibrant, cacophony of Florence. Whenever I descended to the small shops for provisions, I was immediately received with curiosity and myriad of questions, as well as, the mindless chatter of shop vendors fishing for information they could later retail with their tomatoes. Strada in Chianti mirrored all the small towns in Italy with this trait and when later I moved to Apex I found truth in the world view adage that Rina, who had never left Tuscany, would declare;

" Tutto il modo a paese"[2].

Once the butcher in Baccaiano where I worked, a small town outside of Empoli, hoping to pay me a compliment and obtain my loyalty, indirectly asked me my age. I smiled knowing what he was implying and asked,

"Why do you want to know?"

---

[2] "The whole world is a small town."

The shop keeper stammered as he was caught off guard, Kikka poked her fingers into the chickens' cages and tried to feed them her cookies. The Butcher toggled between mother and daughter, a tendency that would accompany Kikka and I most of my designing career. Asking if the toddler wanted "pollo" for dinner and questioning me about my recent pregnancy, the GioMar collection and De Sante Faire. Finally, wanting the game to end and get home after all, I had over a hundred Kilometers before reaching destination, I asked,

"How old do you think I am?"

He smiled, now he had permission to look me over much like he looked over cattle before the purchase. I grew uneasy as I suddenly became aware of the carnal tension between me and the butcher, the sharp knives on the counter and how terribly venerable the situation was- just me and my two year old daughter in the small shop. I felt the acid in my throat and had flashes of a memory that was tucked deep in a damp place of my soul. I must have visibly paled from my thoughts and the butcher, less aggressive and charmed by the curly headed cherub that was sticking her tiny finger into the feathers of the chickens' behind looking for eggs, answered as he prepared an egg for Kikka to drink. "Tieni" he handed the raw egg to my daughter after poking a hole in the end and shaking it vigorously with a bit of sugar and a drop of his espresso,

"Trenta-cinque ma portato benissimo - Thirty-five but carried extremely well."

I gathered my daughter into my arms disgusted by the egg she was sucking from the shell, thanked him and gathered my packages.

"Allora?"

Well? He inquired, I looked at him coldly, "Allora, my ass" I thought. I would become a vegetarian. How it could take forty minutes, for what could be done in a supermarket in the States in two, was beyond me. This "good Momma" business was not for anyone who had a career. That was damn sure! Whatever would I do when I had the twins? Already I did not have enough arms to restrain Kikka and the drive to Baccaiano was enough to send me over the edge, with three car accidents from sleep deprivation and speed, I knew our luck would one day run out.

"Buona Sera." I bid him as I left.

I was twenty-five.

There are two ways of spreading
light-to be the candle or the mirror
that reflects it.

~Edith Wharton

Chapter 12: Forest Friends

Gli Scopeti, Tuscany, Italy 1992

We had been getting farther apart. I was exhausted; now three small children, two au pairs, constant guests that visited our restaurant and the Monday trips all fell on my shoulders. My husband would arrive upstairs after hours of drinking with his buddies drunken and lustful and I would look at the clock and pray that he would leave me alone. I had 4 hours maybe 5 before I had to get up. He would sleep in but I needed to get up to garner the solace and comfort of my walking buddies Roberta and Ginny in the sanctuary of the Scopeti Forest.

Ginny's husband Fulvio Faraone was a lawyer. If something ever happened to me he would make sure my children were taken care of and despite the large Corti clan in Tuscany, Faraone had promised me he would arrange for my children to return to the states. He knew all too well this Ital-Americano situation first hand. He had married a California Oil heiress: Virginia McCloud, "Ginny" .They also had three children, though older and in university when we met. She warned me that money made the distance shorter but without we would have to consider moving back before the children started university. All children she said should experience university life in the States. For this, my children and I will be forever grateful.

> *"Oh Dio, turn the lights off Riccardo!" Malia shrieked.*
> *"Why, the spaghettata is almost ready?" responded the confused waiter.*
> *"Just do it, please I think I hear 'Capello".*

Capello was an amusing, eccentric man who made up for his unattractiveness with an incredible sense of style and up to the minute fashion and trendy accessories. When watch collections were the vogue he not only had the usual suspects: Patek Philippe's and Panerais he would customers traveling to pick up unusual Swatches and vintage Disney character Timex. His premature loss of hair, which one assumes was down the middle of his back at one time, made for the constant companion of a Stetson on his head. The nickname "Capello" which means "hat" was what most people called him. His heart was as big as his Stetson, but his caprices unpredictable and untimely were a constant cause for argument. In fact, after years of frequenting him and his wife Shelley, I never knew if my husband enjoyed his company or what his real name was.

His wife, Shelley was a stunning classic American beauty. Tall and tan, slender and confident her short, blond highlighted hair and steel grey eyes made her uncompromising as much as she was unconventional like her husband. When she walked into a room everyone turned partially for her presence and partially for the unusual couple they made. At a few millimeters under six feet in stockings she towered over her *Italianino* husband.

She was beautiful, he was not but on one ground they stood evenly they could morph into the most menacing of monsters at the tilt of a bottle. When Capello and Shelley came calling usually after the restaurants had closed their kitchens and the clubs were not yet jumping you knew that trouble would follow.

They were the life of the party until they finish the wine drinking and start the grappa. One night my husband pulled me aside and told me that I should probably not ride with Shelley any more, that I could not trust her. Later, I never knew how to act when they came, like many of our patrons grappa is where the switch comes on. It is the switch that makes men push themselves up against you and the switch that makes women put their tongues in your mouth or places they don't even remember. A delirium sets in and a vortex of madness, voices rise and tempers flare no one really remembering why. Expensive bottles go missing and jewelry is lost. It is mind numbing. I just want sleep. I want the smoke to stop and the lights to go out and I do not want the rest of the evening to be a reiteration of what happened, because most of the time I have no idea what just happened.

It is as if the iron curtain has been lowered again leaving me in a language of my own, only to release me later to the interrogator. Some things I remember and I understand. Now at a distance I try to piece together the clues of a puzzle with fuzzy edges and no real color or fit. Was he in pain? Was the accident what changed him or was there always a man inside that I did not know? I remember the warning I received on the cutting floor when I was a young designer.

The Other Side of Tuscany

"You are in love with a very temperamental man; no love is strong enough to put out that fire."

Later he explained why he had punched the man for standing in the street talking to someone in the window.

"I was on my LeMans, I came squealing around the corner and there he was talking to Nadia. I managed not to hit him and not to lie down my bike but when I stopped I got off and punched him. I think I might have knocked his teeth out."

I had seen the curve on the road to Pozzolatico and the Pub that Nadia's parents ran. Her window was directly on the curve above the bar with high stone walls, girdles to the olive groves above, lining the narrow road. I am sure less speed may have also helped make it less dramatic but I did not dare say that. After all, it is a very thin slice of meat that has only one side.

Let us be grateful to the people
who make us happy; they are the
charming gardeners who make our
souls blossom.

~Marcel Proust

Chapter 13: Malia

Gli Scopeti, Tuscany, Italy 1993

Who would have thought that what started as a
simple solution to twins would turn into not only a
lucrative business but the font for many dear people
in our lives? Never would I have guessed that
converting the hidden rooms of our home into a
bistro, we would have a sidewalk café of humanity.
Like us, they also had a front row seat to our daily
drama.

We had been lobbying for a coveted vendor ship
with the Japanese and local tourist bureau. Milo
Kraft, famed Swiss hotelier and food critic, had
counseled us well and pulled strings, as did Leo
Codacci, of the same importance locally. Journalists
and politicians were frequent guests. After a few
years, we had the luxury of opening only on a
reservation basis and this was especially true at
lunch.

That day, the table was perfectly set. Inside the
linen Lotus folded napkins, I had tucked a single
Giuggiole berry[1] with a tiny satin bow.

---

[1] A typical fruit in the Venetian region hard to find in
Tuscany.

"Stronzate" [2] my husband and his cousin, Frank had said at the time. Then, they always seemed to think that of the brushstrokes of imagination I would give to something as uninspiring as setting a table or making a salad. For me, it was survival; it was the thread that connected me to my creative past.

"Brodo di Giuggiole" was an expression in our part of Italy meaning a person was particularly happy. Though the actual broth of Giuggiole (after much research) did not really exist, other than as liquor, I decided to put it on the menu. (That is what people whose moniker is "Malia" do.) Logical enough I thought, great marketing thought everyone else.

The accident could not have been the reason my colleague Nadia thought he was a violent man, that was so many years before. But in the later years I wondered if that was why he changed so much.

I remember having played over and over what I would serve that day. I mentally flipped a rolodex of memories, colors and tastes in my mind. A million combinations, a million insinuations with each one: if it were too Anglo a dish it would seem I had disregard for the region, classic Italian could be a dangerous imitation, and Tuscan lacked flair. I then decided to take the traditional flavors of the very woods we lived in, the Scopeti Forest and combine them in a dangerously incongruous combination.

My husband had been supportive of the repurposing of Porcini Mushrooms with blueberries and local truffles. Important press and tourism contacts were

---

[2] A vulgar, Tuscan expression meaning "foolishness".

visiting San Casciano, Val di Pesa and had requested an exclusive opening of the restaurant for lunch. Orazio added the best, freshest local ingredients - if his family did not produce or gather it, he had a connection. This took a lot of the pressure off me, since only an idiot could ruin food this good (although there have been cases, but I blame an overly agile cork screw.) He could take a simple pizza and change the flavor by adding different woods to the fire when he baked it. He had won me over with his independence in the kitchen and his palate even if the first time I saw him cook he had sugared the Bistecca alle Fiorentina[3] and salted the Crema Marscarpone.[4]

In the kitchen, we were alchemists and artists paying homage to the fruits of Tuscany, together. There was a ceremony and holiness when we had plenty of time for the needed preparation, but it was a pandemonium when we did not.

"We will need the last oven for the bread- it will be perfect. Marconi will have it ready at 11:30 and I will have enough time to get the bread while you serve the Prosecco and 'Salatini.'"

I grew up in a bakery and I knew he was right but how many people can really tell the difference - honestly? I find it hard to believe there are that many of us out there discussing the hour of the bread. Still, he insisted and I felt that uneasiness that happens when you know something terrible is going to happen. Orazio could tell from the look on my face I did not want him to go.

---

[3] The classic T Bone Steak served in Florence that is between 4-6 inches thick.
[4] Double Cream Cheese raw egg custard.

"Nancetti, nothing will happen, serve them the wine crisp and fresh tell them one of your little stories and even if Marconi is a little behind you will be fine."

I loved it when he used his pet name for me but it did not calm me. Florence had been bombed[5] in the early morning hours - Capello's mom had survived only because a beam landed on her Wrought iron bed and in doing so created a cavity that sheltered her from the other two collapsing floors in the apartment in Piazza della Signoria. I was feeling that the moon was not right and I wanted him here with me. We were to do this together. For some reason, I knew we wouldn't be doing this together.

There are memories that are just shadows that become monsters in our minds; something sets the stage of that mind print, a smell, a place, a taste or sound. Something was nagging me now and I was frightened but I did not know what it was. Was it the group of addicts that had pushed me against the stone wall a few nights before when I had been alone, looking for money and water for a fix? Or the drunken patrons that would linger when Orazio would sneak upstairs to catch the last part of a soccer match on television and try to kiss me as I writhed out of their way? Even the mention of needle-dependant robbers, with their haunting, empty expressions, did not stall Orazio; he left.

There were times where my husband pulled me to safety and others times when I felt very alone.

---

[5] May 27th, 1993: a bomb explodes in front of the Georgofili Academy, just by the Uffizi Gallery, killing five innocents in their sleep. Other mafia bombs detonated in other Italian cities that year: for the first time in its history the mafia was attacking the State outside Sicily.

All the while our children slept or played. Our children knew all the languages of past and present. They were old souls the mid wives had told me. They knew how to navigate the folds to safety.

Alone I served the aperitif and danced the delicate dance of the restaurateur who finds herself with no staff: conversation, stir the pot, mingle, arrange crostini, stoke the fire in the fireplace, excuse yourself to get more kindling, turn the roast…

Boom.

Glasses rattled and the side French doors that had been unlocked blew open. We all looked at each other. The men ran outside toward the bridge. One woman used the telephone to call the news agency.

The restaurant is situated in the wine cellar of our 1700 century home at the bend of the mouth to the Scopeti Forest and sits below street level. There is the old mill that is below our home fed by a service road that looks almost as if it is going to pass under our home but it turns and follows the retaining wall to our property and continues along the Greve River. To get to our home you must turn off the Chiantigiana (the boulevard of Chianti) and onto the only stone bridge left intact over the Greve river by the Germans in World War II. After the bridge there is a hairpin curve, to the left is our home and to the right the road continues through the woods to the exile home of Machiavelli, in Saint Andrea in Percussina. From the turn-off, the Chiantigiana to the door of the restaurant is about 200 meters.

The men were met by my very nosey, hysterical neighbor, Cesarina who lived on the other side of the bridge. Her kitchen window strategically looked onto the bridge. She knew all the comings and goings. She had blood on her work smock and she was ringing her hands. They stood on the part of the bridge nearest the gated entrance to our restaurant. They kept looking at me so I decided I was better off tending my meal. I was furious with Orazio, why was he not here? If they did bomb the bridge he was surely standing there looking at all the confusion and probably forgot about the luncheon.

The gnawing in my stomach reminded me of what the doctor had told me. I just did not feel like eating.

The guests did not seem interested in eating either, I just could not understand. Now I was pissed, I had worked so hard to make sure that everything was perfect.

I started to plate up the tiny porcelain terrains with Brodo di Giuggiole and arrange the crostini around it. On the slicer I thinly sliced the cantaloupe and twisted it as if organza. Then I rolled the prosciutto in the same way and placed a sprig of fresh bay next to what now looked like two rare flowers.

"Signora Malia?"

I looked up to see the Carabinieri standing in the doorway between the cellar and the kitchen. Now I am panic stricken. The last thing I needed were more guests or worse, an inspection of sorts with the inevitable "cash contribution."

This would be the last time we would do "bread by the hour."

If you are going through hell, just
keep on going.

~Winston Churchill

Chapter 14: Fear, A Good Thing

Gli Scopeti, Tuscany, Italy1993

It is amazing what we can accomplish, if we refuse
to be afraid. The jaws of life were starting to release
my husband from the wreckage before I could even
start to comprehend what was happening or even
walk the 100 meters to him. My mind, my legs were
just not working. I felt like everyone had decided to
speak in a different language or that someone had
forgotten to set the alarm clock. Yes, that was it, no
need to worry I would be waking soon, this was just
one of my terrible dreams. I could smell the
eggplant burning on the grill it was so real...

"Signora, please come with me your husband wants
to see you before they take him to the hospital. We
have called his sister and she will meet us there.
You can come when you are ready."

Ready for what?

I looked at him and the crowd behind him now
looked at me, as one that looks at the pigeon woman
in the piazza feeding the birds with pitiful
helplessness. On the stainless steel table sat twelve
white porcelain plates with tiny terrenes filled with
a veiled soup and warm, wilted prosciutto e melon.

It was making water and the crusty- once perfect-toast points were now soggy.

"Won't you eat first, it is all ready?"

I asked, clearly in shock, behind me in groups of twelve were the next 3 courses, wilted and ruined on the various work counters of the small kitchen. I had just kept cooking and plating up as if this was not happening.

The Carabinieri came now to me and I could see tears in his eyes. He put his arms on my shoulders as if to squeeze me into a narrower person, the gesture confirmed his uneasiness with the situation.

"You are going to be alright your husband is going to make it, it could have been worse."

He said each word as if he was not sure I could understand English or was mentally challenged. Then Lucia, Frank's wife appeared and said,

"Orazio is *OK;* you can see him before they take him away."

I walked slowly to the crumbled Renault that used to be our extra vehicle for errand running, had he been in the Mercedes this might not have been so bad. The car had been opened like a can without proper tools and my husband was strapped to a body board, his head immobilized by a contraption that looked like it belonged in a magic show act.

No one came to saw my husband in two; still I did not wake up; the man with bunny and hat did not come either. No magic act, just a miracle.

I bent down to kiss him and he grimaced.

"Did you get the bread?" I asked trying to make light of the situation and trying to be strong and not cry.

"You were right; I won't be doing lunch today."

I tried to laugh but no sound came. He tried to smile but only blood trickled from the corner of his mouth.

Orazio would spend less time in the hospital than anyone would have ever imagined that day after seeing the car and the swollen pulp of flesh and blood that used to be the man I married.

I had to move quickly. The children could not know and a friend was picking them up from school that day since we imagined being occupied with a press conference after the elaborate lunch. I too had plans. I had planned on crawling into bed with a sniffer of sauternes and a wedge of gorgonzola after making love to my husband and taking a lovely nap. That was not happening. More importantly, the children would have to pass by the tangled guardrail and gaping hole in the stone wall. They would not only notice, but it would be dangerous, it was the only way to our house without going all the way to San Casciano and then descending the steep hill to the Greve Valley from the other side. With part of the wall missing, they could be driven off into the river below with the slightest inattention.

He healed quickly. His rehabilitation ignored after he regained enough strength to sign himself out of the hospital. He could not be immobilized. There was so much to do and I was trying to keep

❧ The Other Side of Tuscany ☙

everything going seamlessly but he felt I could not be left alone. He knew my fears well and they had foreshadowed a situation neither of us imagined. His injuries would leave him with excruciating pain, insomnia and mood swings for the rest of his life.

I loved my husband dearly. In those days, I felt bitter and cheated. Why did this happen to us? How could changing the channel on the car radio wreak such havoc on my husband's life? How could God have let that happen?

I stood in the parking lot that night while the children slept in their beds, tummies full of a dinner of Uovini Kinder,[1] and asked God why he let this happen. I told him to go to hell. I expected, and silently hoped, he would strike me down in that moment, so that I could rest.

There were so many obstacles and so little help in gathering justice, yet we plugged on. We had to for our children. I cried myself to sleep and took refuge the lofts above the children's rooms; hiding from a man I loved who sometimes scared me.

---

[1] Kinder® Chocolate eggs that are lined with white chocolate and have a plastic egg that contains a small toy, perfect for choking small children. And Italian mothers gave them to their children when there wasn't time for a meal, the kids loving them.

To each other, we were as normal
and nice as the smell of bread. We
were just a family.

~John Irving

Chapter 15: Michele

Gli Scopeti, Tuscany, Italy 1995

The white ceramic bowl came down hard on my
feet sending the tiramisu and its heavy scalloped
edges into a thousand pieces. Though the heavy
pieces struck my toes as if they had been shut in a
door I stood like a statue, tears rolling down my
face not from the pain or the cuts that were now
bleeding into the espresso and cream about my
ankles; but the shame that my children and waiters
had to witness, my life the movie, playing before
them. It was a daily war no one knew was coming,
the enemy creeping up in the guise of the loving
man who once looked like Michael Landon. How
could this have happened? I was always so
organized, kept lists, I could squeeze more hours
out of a day than the expert laundress, a fine linen
sheet. Yet here I was floundering in despair. My
husband was trapped in his anger and pain in a
prison that had become *him*.

The children were not there in the summers, I would
send them to America. It would give me time to
navigate the drama of our daily lives, his mother
running away, her Alzheimer's rampant and out of
control, and my husband unpredictable outbursts,
since the accident on the bridge, was easier to gauge

๕ The Other Side of Tuscany ๙

without the distractions of the children. Still, the children were my only allies with the "new Rina" and Tuscany; I knew they would be better off this way. If anything ever happened there would be no doubt where they would live and they would be ready for a life there. I worried like that.

I missed them terribly and woke most nights not from the sticky heat but the sensation that someone was stealing them from my parents. I feared every child predator in America knew where they lived. My friends back home found this amusing.

"How can you send them to Dayton, Ohio for the summers when they live in one of the most beautiful places on earth? You should have a social worker evaluate your parenting!" they would tease.

These are the same friends who would think I was being dramatic about my life as I would reach out of the chaos for a hand. "He probably just forgot who he was talking to and just hauled off and hit you - for Chrissake, Nac get over it, You live in Tuscany!"

There once was a letter in my writing place. Now that letter and several of the others are gone. I had stated that the children would go to my friend Michele. She was my soul sister and though years and miles would divide us, we were always connected.

She would come and gather the children into her love and protect them and though I would be gone she would spoil and comfort them. Knowing my children, who thought my mysterious friend from college was a princess, would be ok with that even if Mommy had gone away. She popped into their

73

lives bearing gifts more than Christmas, accessorized with the latest gadgets and jewels. Michele Hallahan Power gave new meaning to "with bells on". When Princess Michele arrived, our house turned into a palace, taking my husband back to the simplicity that was our courtship, to a kindness that he had for beautiful blonds with blue eyes, and a grace that was forgotten in the comfort of our marriage.

Was it also because I too became that young girl he knew?

When Michele came to town, dancing and nightlife came back into our lives. My husband would make up "private parties" and close the restaurant so that we could ride the motorcycles down the tree lined boulevard and "people watch" at Piazziale Michelangelo and then ride into the night cloaked streets of Florence, seeking Gelato at Vivoli's and English movies directly in front. Michele and I would reminisce about our time in Europe together; though it had been brief, it was a defining moment in our history and in my life.

Once I had arranged a tour for our school at the factory where I worked in the heart of Chianti. Gandolfo and his daughters, honored to show off their factory and the graciousness that only comes from having blue blood, welcomed my former classmates with pastries from Sarti and lavish gifts. The greatest gesture being that I could return with them to Florence and stay with my friend Michele in the hotel and chat all night. Little did they know our plans included Orazio and his best friend, Alessandro, Sandro for short.

The Other Side of Tuscany

Sandro who had met Michele on that school trip from London would sheepishly arrive at our house every time she came to visit every year after. In my heart, I always hoped the two of them would end up together. How my life would have been different! Though her mother, Marlene would have hated having her daughter half way around the world, Sandro would have given her the life she deserved. And the children she did not have.

I vicariously lived the career I had aborted for the love of my children and husband through her, thinking one day my life would start again. I would mark on a calendar when I thought that would be. The date was near the one where I calculated the next time I would sleep again after the twins had been born. It was far away, and it was nearly impossible, but it was a date nonetheless and some days I felt that was all I had.

Michele understood and told me in vivid details about the lines she was building and the shopping she was doing in order to tear apart and copy the clothes she had purchased abroad. Together we would incorporate the colors and textures into my restaurant not in the décor but in the food, taking tidbits from Cal a Vie and Martha Stewart. Michele had brought Martha Stewart into my life when middle America did not even know who she was.

That spring break night in Florence 10 years earlier, Orazio and Sandro had waited for us, as we returned from Yub-Yum[1] in our strappy heels and original designs; un-hemmed and damp from our dancing, to take us back to spend the night together in a suburb of Florence where Sandro had a flat.

---

[1] Popular Discothèque in Florence.

Michele had asked me to pack a huge flannel nightgown that Zia Teresa had given me. "Why" was the operative word as the thick English Flannel gown packed in a satchel made me to look like a "bag lady" in the club but I did not argue, Michele was good about things like this. Later, when we arrived she quickly removed all the sexiness and put on the gown. As she walked around the apartment while Orazio and I giggled and kissed, I remembered thinking how subtle she had been to not offend Sandro's ego. How was it she knew the prairie gown would make her look like a vintage porcelain doll too precious to touch?

Michele always knew.

അൽ

"Ma che fai?" "What are you doing?"

Riccardo came rushing into the kitchen. Silvia and Nicolo' knew better to get involved and had walked back into the dining area.

It was difficult, their position, Silvia had been my friend and Nicolo', Orazio's. When they became a couple it was difficult to navigate the roles. Now, they were also our employees and rented our guest house. I did not blame them.

I stood. I could no longer feel my toes, and Riccardo looked up at me as he tried to clean up my wounds and make me laugh. He asked if I would like to make a strawberry garnish to hide the blood in the Tiramisu.

"Si ricicle?" We recycle? He asked. "I could scoop it and you could garnish with one of those fancy little *thingmajobs* you do? Hell it will be so pretty when you are done we could probably still leave the broken dish in it!" He continued. I stood still.

"When did he become like this?"

Riccardo looked at me as if willing the answer, or was he just making an excuse for a man he cared for deeply. Riccardo was good at that; he had had a lifetime of experience with his own family.

CB&SO

The Carabinieri was telling me, "It's Orazio."

I was not registering what the Carabinieri were saying; it just did not make sense why would my husband be in a car with a bomb.

There was no bomb.

"The bomb" was my husband's car slowing down to turn and cross the bridge when he was hit, at rocket force by a teenager changing the channel on the radio and not seeing the slowed car. This thrust the car after impact into the guardrail in front of our neighbor, Cesarina's home causing the explosive sound.

The boom was the sound of impact bouncing off the canyon walls that cradled our lives, the bridge and my husband tethered by twisted metal.

That day, as the accident rocked the hamlet leaving scars on the stucco faces of century old structures, our Tuscany also changed. Orazio, healthy and strong, appeared to be fully recovered in a few weeks despite constant pain and an inability to sleep.

We, the children and I, have never recovered from that day.

 𝄞𝄢

Then I looked at the green plastic skids that Michele had suggested. She had seen them in the kitchen at the Golden Door, as they also had Terracotta floors. She had said it would be would be easier on our legs and definitely "kinder" to our feet, if we placed them on the terracotta floor in our kitchen. She had been so convinced about it that she sent pictures from every angle so that Orazio could find the right ones or type of material to make them if need be.

Regardless of what Michele or the manufacturer said, my feet were killing me.

Michele was good like that and it is not her fault that she did not calculate the flying dessert terrenes. I laughed.

I can laugh about things like this because I live in Tuscany, just on the other side.

Discontent is the first step in
progress. No one knows what is in
him till he tries, and many would
never try if they were not forced to.

~Basil Maturin

Chapter 16: First Step Out

Gli Scopeti, Tuscany, Italy 1995

My husband and I were more and more at odds. His
constant sleeping and my never sleeping lead to
arguments over things that we never much thought
of before.

"Why do I have to go to the Christmas play!?! You
go and I will run the restaurant. I know all those
songs by heart." I would say.

"I go to the soccer games. You go to the school
stuff." He would reply.

"*But* you like to go and I would like to go and watch
the kids play once in a while, besides the nuns hate
me there."

"They don't hate you, they just think you are odd
and a heathen ever since you thought they went on
strike like the rest of Italy."

We would go on for hours sometimes it ended well
and other times, not so well. It only fueled gossip
when one of us was not present at a function or
worse, to be overheard arguing in the town square,

later our discussions retailed with the home growth produce.

Unintentionally, but inescapably, the fascination of *Malia* was mainly driven by my enemies. In doing so, they defeated their mission to diminish me by making my existence larger than life, my faults those reserved for women without milk in their breasts or hearts in their chests. As far as I was concerned, since everyone had their own versions of the "truth" when I could I fueled, the fire. Humorously, contradicting and discredited my critics, making me all the more adorable I went to great lengths in making fools out of those weaving the stories.

"Well of course, I was a hooker and that exemplifies what a resourceful wife I was… charging my husband for his sexual depravities….just because *she* can afford to accommodate him for free….well I guess that would make her - how do you say, *Cheap?*"

And my audience would erupt into laughter at the absurdity of the claim. But then I would add with intension and look them straight in the eye, "Calculate. How I could have raised my three small children, care for my mother in law and run our restaurant while my husband worked in Siena? I am not a super hero."

Then, there would be silence. That moment of easiness, of equality with me had evaporated; I had a way to cut you to your quick with my heart-felt righteousness- just ask any smokers in Italy. You never wanted to get on the wrong side of my crusade or it was going to be hell to pay.

The Other Side of Tuscany

Orazio liked that about me in the beginning. He liked that I had the fight in me to get out of every traffic violation and turn every augment into an education. Then I became strange to him, my earnest not as authentic and in the end, the smoke we detested together only seemed to bother me.

He suspected this love; our love was too good to last and managed to brood whenever he doubted me. Why had he not confronted me with the rumors and nip them in the bud? Or was he afraid I would berate the wagging tongues with a few lashes of my own? Were these rumors only in the years after I left Italy, the rumor mills were swaddled in the protection of my absence, safe from my rebuttals?

At the insistence of friends and family that had always felt threatened by me, he began to stray. It was ok, it was to be expected, after all he was a man. A woman's indiscretions are sins; a man's are only science.[1]

"What do you think she is doing?" These questions were backed with facts and figures and even personal testimony. So that made it "alright", that sanitized the dirtiest of sins just like confession absolves the murderer with a few rounds of "Hail Mary."

At first, it was just in spurts without importance, he had told me, just sexual escapes. Then there were other players in this game, the husbands and children abandoned for promises of a life together where they were no longer desired. How I wanted to comfort these discarded players. I knew what it was

---

[1] It is thought that men biologically need to have sex, whereas women can take it or leave it. This thinking absolves men from infidelity but not women.

like to not be on the "A" team. And then the collection assembled "surrogate" wives. Smoking, surrogate wives, ashes to asses is no Roman mass much less a Roman holiday, wrong film. This was a Tuscan tale taking Francis' sun kissed story and making mine the cheap *Ballywood* remake.

I was getting bitter and feeling sorry for myself. Cheated and looking for someone to blame and someone to pay but not having the fight in me.

Somewhere between the wedding planning and the child bearing the iron curtain is lowered. The women remain with their girlfriends and sisters, the men with their friends and lovers... and the children scramble for cover. Where in the cycle of an Italian courtship does the curtain come down? When is it the players become complacent and the unraveling and the escapes soon forgotten?

One day an iron curtain was dropped in the middle of my Tuscan life. The light no longer shined on my dreams. My stilettos packed and wooden clogs replaced them. I wanted to strut but it was all I had to keep the children growing in the limited light.

One day it was decided. I took them to America where we would rebuild our lives and Orazio would join us and prove all the naysayers wrong: we were the "coppia piu bella dell' mondo"[2].

Though I saw it lowering, so tumultuous were the years after the twins arrived and Rina, that as I scrambled, I lost track of what side I was on. Orazio never came and with each year that passed, the

---

[2] Popular Italian Love song by Celentano, "The Most Beautiful Couple in the World" and it continues with "we are so sorry for the rest of you..."

curtain that separated us became thicker. Now I was on the "other side" by default.

A man can be happy with any
woman as long as he does not love
her.

~*Oscar Wilde*

Chapter 17: The Cross We bear

Apex, North Carolina, USA 1998

I had always planned on coming back to America
with the children one day so that they could go to
American university. This plan was known to all
that took the time to ask, our clients, our friends and
some family. It was known but not understood,
since to those that live in Italy, in is impossible to
think of living anywhere else. Imagine the surprise
to my husband when he was told by one of his
college buddies that that this was always the plan
and he just did not remember.

Not that I did not appreciate the beauty and the
culture Tuscany afforded us, but because before the
technology boom, Italy was behind North America
in opportunity, technology and diversity. When
Europe started with attaching to technology it was
easier to skip generations and go directly to the
newer advances rather than a traditional
progression. While it was excelling in some areas
there was a close mindedness with religion, race
and basic liberties that should be afforded all people
especially women. Not the environment I wanted
for my children. By the time they had finished
Middle School, I felt the best that Italy could give

them before it could take it away, had been absorbed.

My husband supported me when I started visiting cities across America looking for the perfect spot. When I settled on North Carolina many were surprised, especially my friends and family that were stateside. In North Carolina, I knew not a single soul. I decided that was a good thing. I had no trouble adapting in London and the situation was much the same. Now, I would be coming with two of my three children and my husband and Kikka would follow once a home and livelihood were secured.

Never would I have guessed moving to a country where one was born and reared for sixteen years, you could feel so foreign. My mother tongue was morphed into a whole new set of rules and restrictions. Though my children and I spoke perfect English there were things that were no longer said even offensive. People were mindful of our not belonging and while welcoming if we joined them at their church, not so kind if we insisted on staying at ours. I had thought all the boxes that confined me in Italy would be released once I came back to my country; instead they had followed me home.

Two years in America as a divided family, passed almost as swiftly as the trip itself. While my eldest joined us after a year, my husband did not. That image of the bridge that joined the two countries stronger than ever on my wish list... But even if it would exist, I never had a day off where I would have been able to walk it, even if only half way to the middle. I worked two jobs and picked up as much overtime as I could. The more I thought about the bridge the more I realized that my husband would not walk to the middle. If he had not come to America, he certainly would not walk across a bridge even if one side of it was safely on his Italian shore.

I had too much imagination he had said when I told him my thoughts out loud.

"Mette i tuoi piedi per terra…put your feet on the ground and think like the rest of us. You need to make enough money that I can come over and pick it up with a wheel barrel and then I will come but for now, I have to be stable because you clearly are not."

I realized that if Orazio were here, I would be able to work 10 hours less a week, such was the expense of our phone bill. I realized if Orazio were here, I would not have to pay someone to take one of the twins to soccer while the other came with me. I realized if Orazio were here with me, Kikka would not hate me so much. Her year in Italy had left deep scars not just for being the housewife to my husband, but for all the vicious words she had to hear.

"What type of mother do you have that she leaves *you* behind? Are you from another marriage? Which do you like better here or there? You will get fat in America they all are…You know there are a lot of Black people in North Carolina…" They pelted her like unexpected summer hail in the midst of sunbathing.

Our savings were quickly diminishing as more activities required that I clone myself through paid friends and acquaintances. There were things to help you the bank had said. My problem was I had no credit. They would help me through credit cards with high interest rates, but in the end I would have a good rating and could get even more credit cards.

Not that I had bad credit, which later I would understand was actually better than no credit at all. Having lived my entire adult life abroad had left me completely unprepared for being an alien without a credit rating. I had money but apparently that was not worth half as much as a rating. God bless those who navigate this bureaucracy without having language on their side.

E-mail would prove to be a blessing and a curse. Letting information and people come into my life like a stray cat at the door, that you feed and wish would go away. Yet you continue to feed it. I poured my heart out to perfect strangers in this new strange world and they in turn would collect it and look for more chances to feed at my door. The love poems, the bedtime stories and the promises to rescue me from my personal limbo.

With the e-mail came technologies and wonderful new millionaires popping up all over the country selling two lines of code or an idea on the back of a napkin for millions of dollars. I gathered my wheelbarrow and with a neighbor decide to build the bridge I desired by creating virtual property tours. In that way, we could sell our properties from here and go there, just when it was needed to close the deal. Orazio, though he did not even know how to turn on a computer on his own, supported and funded the angel round. He believed if I put this much passion into something I knew nothing about, it surely it would make money, much like our restaurant years before.

I pushed on hoping to fill the wheel barrel so that I could gather my husband and unite our family. I was lonely and I was angry. This was not the plan. I had raised the children almost alone in Italy and I could not deal with the challenges of a globalized family unless everyone knew how to use e-mail. With each sales presentation of our product, I slowly realized that not everyone had the need to shrink the world like I did. I would show up excited and convinced to have the next e-Bay, only to spend 2 hours explaining what e-mail was and no, "we don't come and install that for you."

As another year passed, I was no closer to having my family together. That year, my birthday fell on Easter. I wanted to celebrate. As a little girl when my birthday fell on Easter, I was dressed as a rabbit and taken to Good Samaritan Hospital to pass out cookies to the sick children. It made me happy to be so special that I could do that. I felt something good would happen that year; instead I had that familiar feeling of dread, like when you forget something on a trip but are not really sure what it is..

My children were too young to know the difference other than remember it was either Easter or my birthday. My husband to this day cannot remember when my birthday is. I set my expectations low and went in to work the morning breakfast shift at the Marriott. Imagine my surprise when my husband called, and my manager passed me the phone. She was happy; I had just told her how happy I would be if my husband once remembered my birthday.

He had not remembered my birthday. He was having Easter dinner with his cousins from Siena. They seemed so distraught over their own recent incident of infidelity to exaggerate any indiscretions that we may have had. I could sense he was angry but could not understand why. If anyone should be angry it should have been me. Singlehandedly raising our children, working on my birthday and having to rush home to prepare Easter dinner; while he luxuriate over a meal of truffled tagliatelle and roasted lamb with white wine and artichokes. Misery does love to drag company along but why was I folded into their personal drama?

"I want an annulment," my husband of 17 years, and father of my three children, was saying.

Stunned, I held the phone to my ear, no words came from my mouth only tears filled my eyes.

"Nancetti, I will call you later… you are at work…sorry."

Sorry? Was he apologizing for calling me at work when he just asked me for an annulment?

 C8ဆၢ

There are blessings in life that look like blame, bibles that book-end lies and annulment that simply saves inconvenient wives from inexplicable circumstances or death. Am I lucky or just incredibly obtuse to the rules?

This is one of the mysteries of the cross. How many times had I followed the wall and all the bas relief works of the artists feeling *His* pain, as our pain, the church women and me?

"Se ognuno portasse in piazza la sua croce per cambiarla....alla fine riprende la sua perche' sa come portarla." If every one of us brought "our crosses" (our trials and tribulations) to the town square to exchange for someone else's, we all would leave with our own, because we know how to handles ours."

I could not understand the fine lines that are drawn in the flour on the kitchen floor when a man asks you for an annulment. It would be years before this all made sense to me. I thought I had failed at being a wife so terribly, that I was now being erased. Is that what we learn to accept- annulment -as the Happy Birthday that never comes?

No annulment is not an option; tell the Catholic slut you are sleeping with to go away. I will stay married to you until death do us part.

That is what I had learned to do "carry my cross" I only hoped my cross was not to be passed on to my children.
I never again felt that happiness that the bunny had bringing cookies to the hospital children despite how hard I tried to remember their smiles, despite how many birthdays fell on Easter thereafter. The pain is always there.

Happy Birthday. Happy Easter. Happy Annulment, 'til death do us part...

To have great pain is to accept that
we also have great heart, amor
prossimo and generally give a
damn- I think I would not want to
be any other way despite the
consequences.

~Nac

Chapter 18: Finding Pictures

Apex, North Carolina, USA 1998

I did not want to be here but some things you have to do. Clean the infection from the wound or it will stink. This stunk alright, my family had called that day to wish me a Happy Birthday and though all were told of my conversation with Orazio, they continued confused with their pleasantries. They continued like Martha Stewart did that day with her salad. Truth is hard in perfect families and best left in the drawer.

My husband had come a few months later for his "visit" and acted like the annulment question had never come up. I had not forgotten though it would be years before I understood really what it meant and why he had asked out of the blue. He too kept things in drawers. I kept them on my breast, like a crusader's breast plate. Either way they never go away in the light or in the dark. They are always in the damp places where love lived once.

ꝯ⸾ꝸ

Gli Scopeti, Tuscany, Italy1998

I opened the dresser drawer with a long rusty nail that had once held the original roof trellis in place of our Tuscan home. The disarray, of what used to be my bedroom, did not encourage me to look for the key that served as the handle to my 17th century, walnut chest of drawers.

How long had it been? Two years? Three? It looked like one hundred. How could he be so unconventional in his housekeeping?

Then it occurred to me – before we had been married his mother was his personal keeper. Not that he was some mamma's boy, that just was the Italian way. Never had he or any Italian male that still had a mamma alive; have to worry about any of their belongings. When a woman marries an Italian male, she becomes his keeper and with that, a lack of gratitude and compliment, only duty. In trying to fill the shoes of mamma all attempts at getting it right are futile. When I left for America, that task was left to burden my eldest daughter, Kikka, who had resentfully fallen into the replacement role.

I dipped into the piles of dusty photographs, the dust making me itch and sneeze but still I continued. I needed to reassure myself of a past I was part of and in some way, a protagonist. I needed to reassure myself that I did in fact, exist at one time.

I was solemn as if in prayer when I came upon the pictures of our vacations. I was always in the limelight yet the pictures that captured those moments were few to remind me. I was the historian and with that the caregiver and planner and caterer and navigator. Sadly, there were few pictures, not enough arms; I remembered fondly trying to juggle the twins to take a picture of Kikka on the Island of Lilies. That summer, a kind fellow tourist seeing my obvious disadvantage; two small children in my arms and one climbing on a marble fountain monument to catch a stray cat, had offered to take a picture for us, *per ricordo*. The gentleman was from another part of Italy and while his intent was genuine, his lack of camera skill was such that our *ricordo* was a blurry close up of his face.

The pictures I found were sent from other vacationers on our trips. The beautiful photographs were as if of another couple, taken through a lens that was filtered with admiration and maybe, a bit of envy. Their photographs would accompany polite correspondence after the vacations had finished and the return to the drudgery began.

With guests, I felt so safe, safe from a husband who often scared me and challenged these vacations, so much that after a while I stopped trying to make them happen and sent the children off on their own. These were the times where I could laugh and remember who I was and be sure that it was alright. I could dance and he would watch through a lustful and jealous eye. I could discuss politics and current events. My views were often challenged; yet still I would be heard and not reprimanded because these strangers did not matter to our Tuscan life and the tiny Imprunetean[1] world of my husband's.

Later, in the evening on those vacations, he would make love to me while saying how silly I was and

---

[1] Impruneta was the village that my husband was from. There sins and celebrations are placed (like all small towns) under a magnifying glass.

how stupid the others thought my views were, how inappropriately I was dressed and how unbecoming my hair and make-up was.

The photographs held the truth and not his chiding words.

The years of repressing my spirit were now over.

So why was I here? Kindling a love that he no longer felt? Filling an obligation? I would tell everyone I still loved him, and more, that I always would.

The truth was that the boy I fell in love with, and the man I was married to, were two terribly different people. Unfortunately, they lived in the same sepulcher: my husband. That beautiful Italian boy was taken from me a long time ago. Was it the alcohol and bitterness encouraged by a family that took advantage of him and his mother? That's what I wanted to believe, now I was faced with another possibility: insanity?

As I looked about the room, I knew there was more to coming home than a simple yearning to be his wife. Was he preparing me for death, mine? his? ours? It was something he was never quite capable of when they were together but he had too often mentioned; that way no one would ever have me.

Our bedroom looked more like an arsenal than a romantic retreat, contrasted only by the large Turkish style water bed and large mirror as its head board. It was obvious to anyone who entered their bedroom that more than books were consumed here, even though there were piles of them about the room. His lovers may have smoked after sex but I

The Other Side of Tuscany

read from the many books now scattered, never reading one book at a time, especially not after making love.

"Nessuno fa cosi - nobody does that," he felt compelled to tell me. He often criticized me for reading books from the back and more than one at a time.

"Well I'm not 'NO-body'," I would retort.
And secretly I wanted to say, "Miss No-body" reads one book at a time because she can't hold her fucking cigarette otherwise.

I had no proof even though I could smell stale smoke and found an intimate wash that I was sure my husband did not buy, along with the massage oils and homeopathic ointments in the bathroom cupboard.

I wasn't paranoid, I was tired. There was little of the fight left in me. I just wanted to get our children to a safe spot to weather the storm.

I looked out the window. How many afternoons had I sat at the window and, like the princess locked in a tower in a far away land, prayed for the prince to come and rescue me?

This haven high above the Greve River, the Classic wine path through Chianti hosted many a lazy afternoon where wine and sex encouraged the weaving of arms and legs, sweat and hair that braided the past and present into passionate coupling. Exhaustion would make sense of it all, as we would fall asleep in each other's arms.

95

Then I found a journal page faded and blotted from the tears that had fallen. One I wrote to whoever would find it after my death, in my writing desk. It was written when I was sick. I was having seizures and fainting. The doctors could not place what was wrong with me and the abnormal brain scan had implied there was a tumor.

Benji had found me on the floor one afternoon after rising to answer the phone. I had answered and then fainted. When the caller called back he had answered and told the caller I was "dead."

Translated from the journal page in Italian:

I look at the street below painted with the sunflowers and yellow broom brush, the vineyards and all the perfumes dancing before my eyes. I feel the knocking on the drawer of my desk but I keep it closed and I close you (my writing) there as well .I can't open it, all my life, love will rush out and not live in a place so difficult to survive. But this difficulty is within me, and here in the writing place, you are safe.

The logical voices quelling the contrary... they tell me to close the drawer quickly, to be careful....much as I am fire, I have lived as water. I have wished to be the ocean, the Atlantic, so that I might touch both of the countries I love and live in peace. The fire within me keep will burn all I love. I am distant to keep you safe out of my passion's way. And for this I am sad.

I love you. I love this journey, as much as, I hate it. Together it seems one will stop the other from existing. For every minute I have lived with you, I have died with you.

I was never clever enough, I was never good enough, I was never anything- enough- for you. You told me I was different and while you liked that, you doused the fire with water for being so. Now that I am sick, you are almost happy.

The problem would be solved with my death and then we both would be free. I fight and continue to fight to be well for them- my children.

Open the drawer, find the key, find me, will them to life the dreams, my children, our dreams. I do not want them to be like you- full of the darkness and death. This darkness is what is killing me. My sickness is willed to me by your loathing of life. Please don't take the children to the cemetery at Christmas, only tickle me with your kites.

Then I remembered when I wrote it. A chill comes over me. When the medication was so strong, I merely floated from one day to the next. My writing place was near the window high in our bedroom, in the part of the house that was four stories high. In opening the window, one could easily fall out. Below was the hard, hand-chiseled pattern of granite that formed a perimeter around our home. I had thought about "falling out" if the CAT scan confirmed the worse. I wanted to live, to thrive, and not just exist. A horrible dream a few nights later played out my plan but instead of certain death, I looked up from a puddle of my former self, to see my children crying at the window. I closed the writing place that day and moved it to my studio, only two stories high.

97

CR&O

I removed a stack of pictures. They were from one of our best vacations in the mountains. The children were young, the twins incredibly small. Valtour[2] had been expensive, but so worth it! We had tried other places, since my husband always listened to those envious of our travels. The price tag discredited our obvious pleasure, so occasionally would alternate with a great bargain suggested by the jealous friends, to make up for all the money I had "wasted". After a few, nightmarish attempts in resorts Mussolini's men would have frequented, Orazio allowed me to get my way. Still, I paid for the trips from my earnings, and lied about the cost, to not hear his complaints.

Now looking at the children beaming back at me, Benji with all his accessories and the girls with clown paint, as sun-block, I knew I had been right. These were the vacations that left us totally feeling renewed. These were the vacations that allowed me to remember who I was and allowed my husband to fall in and out of love with me like a day of dirty sex. My husband and I had so much time ourselves, a rarity in the lives of restaurateurs with children. The children skied and skied well, having learned correctly from the start rather than spend 20 years of their life learning to correct poor habits, like us.

Our last one, the vacation at Pila, was pressed into the memory of my children like snow angels on a winter lawn. We had participated in every activity we could, the arm wrestling, the races, the dress up contests and the dance competition, almost as if I knew I would never come back again. The children

---

[2] The Italian club equivalent to Club Mediterrané, an all-inclusive resort vacation package.

had seen their mother as he had seen me; as a fierce competitor, a generous friend with a childlike force of energy.

Maybe this was the reason I was able to last so long? Like a solar battery I recharged economically just enough to keep working but not enough for the flames to raise and start cooking.

Some people move our souls to
dance. They awaken us to a new
understanding, leave footprints on
our hearts and we are never the
same.

~ Nac

Chapter 19: Heart Language

Raleigh, North Carolina, USA 1999

The soccer fields were still damp from the dew
when the loudspeaker summoned an Italian
Interpreter to soccer field number seventeen. I
smiled at the thought of an Italian and their
superstitions about seventeen. I made a mental note
to include cultural numerology in the diversity
packets for the world games next time.

I thought back to when Kikka was born and I was in
the bed that should have been number seventeen
and instead it was 16-B, again I felt I had not made
the "A" series even the bed confirmed it was so.

The injured athlete, a mid fielder from San Marino
had been waiting patiently for over an hour before
the logistics team had realized that they needed
someone who spoke Italian and not French. One of
the downsides to an organization that benefits from
the goodwill of volunteers is there is no assurance
as to the quality, just the good intentions.

I was first generation Italian. Born in America to
Italian, immigrant parents, my mother by boat, and
my father via cargo plane. My mother was from the

South and my father was from the North, though of one country, they did not speak the same language. It was for this my Italian was more of a cacophony of words whose origin drifted in and out as tides and morphed into a language that was *their own language* in the Stolfo household.

While not correct by any means *this language*, not Italian not French not English or Arabic or Polish or Yiddish had a powerful communication that I would pass on to my children. In *our language* was the power to understand the person in front of you. In our language there were no borders, and gates opened with eyes.

I had lived abroad most of my life while my Italian was more Florentine than classic, it was the "tongue of Dante" and it made me uniquely qualified to translate for small town Italy.

I was annoyed when I realized the delay and the very swollen injury were due to ignorance and not scheduling. I was proud to be American but not in these instances.

How could one of the most powerful countries in the world be so sheltered, so shallow, so geographically challenged? I would cringe at Americans' lack of knowledge, even my best friends, in areas of geography and languages. Something I never would quite get over when I lived abroad. Unless there was a war, Americans just could not be bothered with any part of the world that was not *"their own"*. Even the most simple of farmers in Italy knew the great masters, Dante and geography even if they had never left their town in their entire lifetime.

It saddened me to think how many other athletes were maybe getting knees wrapped instead of groins and not getting what they need because they were not understood. I felt my cheeks grow warm as I realized my disapproval was probably scribbled across my face and my disgust evident.

Languages are a strange thing: in love or in need there is no school needed. The heart always understands. I thought of my first walk with Orazio after much secrecy and planning, I obtained permission to have chaperoned runs and long nature walks.

I had purposely walked earlier and earlier, and faster and longer so that I could get through the list of volunteers that Gandolfo's daughters had lined up for me. They were starting to see me a bit more human and less of a stray cat. Since my weight loss I was of even greater value to them, as I could model the collection and the girls could also have a bit more freedom under this pretense.

That morning, was Valentine's Day when Orazio first came to call. He was prepared; as everyone had warned him on how dreadful it was, as I was quiet and persistent on running the hills.

He had brought Yago, a kind German shepherd just in case he could not keep up, to send ahead with me.

To his surprise, that morning I had strolled along side him and in my language, French, and a soft, cautious whisper of Italian, had made small talk. Later, he would tell me that he could not understand me not so much because of my words, but because he was mesmerized by my sultry voice and sensual pursed lips as I tried to perfectly pronounce my new

words for him. He stopped me as we walked across a bridge over the Greve with the farm of Luganno hovering on the hill above,
"Mi peace" thinking it meant "You like me." He said and my eyes grew wide. Who would have said something to him, I wondered.

"Mi peace" He repeated and I was furious, damn it had to have been Fabio he must of said that I liked him. I shot back in Italian,
"Who told you!?!"

And so it when back and forth until Orazio finally pulled my face towards him and kissed me sweetly but for a very, long time.

"Now do you understand?" he finished slowly.

What would dance with me most of my Tuscan life was proper grammar and pesky reflexive verbs. What I had thought meant "You like me" was really, "I like you".

I realized I was smiling at my memories and the little boy was smiling back. I looked intently into the almond shaped eyes, large golden brown eyes flecked with grey. Though the shape of his eyes gave the little guy the look of someone who just rolled out of bed, his face could not have been more alert and solar.

The paramedics told her, "Ask him to take off his shoe, he won't let any of us touch it, then ask him if it is his foot or his ankle."

I quickly translated holding the eyes of the confused child who had started to relax in my gaze.

"Sono nuovi, mi ha comprato la mamma, sono i miei."

The Medical team looked inquiringly at me as if to say" Well?" I offered verbatim the child's reply,

"They are new my mother bought them for me; they are mine."

I smiled again as I realized the boy's origin was probably not from S Marino but my own Tuscany. Not even Down's Syndrome can extract the Tuscano from "Toscannachi!"

I tried again this time adding, "Your Mamma loves you so much, she brought you the best shoes, the fastest shoes"

I knew I was breaking the rules by adding my own editorial but I also knew if I didn't, I would never get the shoes off the little boy and his foot was visibly swollen. The shoes came off, and the medical personnel were able to work quickly and efficiently.

The boy relaxed, he wanted only to talk to me after that.. His coach came over and asked if I could come and watch the second Game that afternoon. I radioed in my position and was given the go-ahead. The earlier snafu needed to be rectified with some sort of reassurance and good one-on-one PR.

I knew what to do when dealing with Italian families: pull on their heart strings find a connection but more importantly, have them forget the earlier incident and replace it with a pleasant thought. If not, we would never hear the end of it.

๒ The Other Side of Tuscany ๙

When I arrived on the sidelines the little boy announced to everyone, "That's my pretty Italian Lady!"

I acknowledged the small group of parents and coaches. I assumed they had come for vacation in America and the world games. A trip to America was an expensive endeavor. I later found out that most of the athletes were alone.

"Sono Malia" I am Malia, I announced using my Italian moniker," sono l'interpretor per La Squadra Italiana Special Olympics." [1]

I finished with American words spoken the American way and Italian words clumsily spoken in their cadence in the same sentence. This always shocked people but it was the melding of who I was and how I always communicated.

" Ma sei Americana or Italiana? "What are you American or Italian?" a woman from Le Spezie asked. The group took their time warming up to me. Alternating their looks from the field to me and then back again. Peppered with a question of two, some related to the games and some to my personal life.

Italians do not have a politically, correct gene in their bodies. They can size you up pound per pound and tell you more about your physical appearance than your own mother, not in malice just for the benefit of your knowing.

Then without warning a woman who had taken a critical distance randomly offered, "Lo sapi che Romina e Al Bano son lasciati?" You know Romina

---

[1] "The interpreter for the Special Olympics Italian Team."

and Al Bano[2] have broken up?" The backhanded words cut me like a knife.

Language is a beautiful and harmful thing. A kind word can make the day seem brighter and a rude one can swiftly take it away. Special are the people that mind the language and the words as if they were their gardens. They are careful to groom the rows and collect the blooms.

Why the woman would want to hurt me after all I did to help her athletes, was beyond me. She knew I would connect Romina to myself, Romina Power being the daughter of Tyrone Power.

Romina beautiful and talented, scrutinized and criticized was more Italian than most of them. Yet that was never enough if you were not born there. When you were considered, "Straniera[3]" you were for life. I had felt her critics as if they were my own. When your tongue is not the tongue of the land of your blossoms you must till the land twice as hard before you are understood and a language becomes your own.

Being from a place does not give you belonging. Just as having a homeland, is not really what you can call home.

---

[2] **Al Bano and Romina Power** were an Italian pop music duo formed by then-married couple Albano Carrisi and Romina Power. They are best known for their songs "Felicità", "Sempre sempre", "Nostalgia Canaglia", and "Libertà". The two separated in 1999.
[3] In Italian this means *stranger* and is used in the same context we use *Alien.* We have a saying in Italian that says, "The world is really the same town..." In all fairness, being called alien is not exactly the height of hospitality either.

Richness is the ability to give not
of our possessions but of ourselves
and while my accountant would
argue, I knew I was the richest
people on the planet.

~Nac

Chapter 20: Counting in Black and White

Apex, North Carolina, USA 2004

I look down at the heaped pages, match books and travel vouchers with thoughts scribbled in a variety of languages and calligraphy. I can smell the situation in which they were received or written. I see the sketches from a life I only visited briefly but lived in my dreams so many nights after I retired.

Some are the letters of a time before electronic mail when recollections were not instantaneous prints but rather the summation of an afternoon set aside to reconnect, like a painter and his canvas, with a ceremony our children will never know. These brush strokes are the painting of a period of my life that is a spiritual journey of forgiveness, rebirth, and self-knowing.

Gemma and I argued after going to the frame shop.

"You don't have the money!" My daughter screamed at me accusingly.

Why did a perfectly sunny Saturday have to be

reduced to a negative number on my bank statement? Why did my daughter have to constantly frame our lives with the black and white of numbers? Why did my daughter see balances, that were measurable only to accountants and bill collectors… and my husband, when taking inventory of what I had accomplished in my life?

Life cannot be measured like that. Life as everything worth doing, needed to be measured in depth.

 I look at the dashes on gravestones and wonder if there could not be a picture instead? A visual to the life lived within that little line. So important yet so insignificant in its record. It makes me sad to think my kids don't see the dash as I do. They may always think of life as year-end statements, as a measure for what counted, or needed to be counted. Though they have learned the lessons too early of what it means to lose a life, time is not as precious at Twenty as it is at Fifty. They cannot measure as I do.

It was true, I did not have the money but what could my daughter understand of the childlike decisions I often made? My children often disapproved of the decisions I mad e- the Christmases celebrated by the unknown children so they would have a bit of light in their lives, only on that day; , the athletes who gobbled down plates of cold pasta after nights of preparation; the hula hoops and trampolines purchased instead of furniture and clothes. Decidedly, I was not like other moms and was "crazy" in my outlook on life.

And, I was a real looser on the balance sheet their father kept.

It's a rainy night in Georgia and I feel like it is raining all over the world..."

The song droned on and I felt comfort in the words remembering my college days in Georgia.

The sadness I felt was almost comforted by the melancholy of the music. I wanted to sing out with him to let him know that I too felt his pain and we were together in this, Georgia or not.

I decided singing out was not a good idea. That really would have given Gemma "pause" to my level of sanity. Already I was "smirking," a habit of late, that I could not seem to control; another trait inherited from my father, that made even innocence seem impossible when the smirk appeared from nowhere mid-argument or thought.

Was freedom worth the mundane of everyday survival? Was freedom worth not knowing if you could bluff through the next set of birthdays or Christmas? Who would secretly pay for Gemma's soccer, save her the embarrassment of another bounced check? What would my excuse be this year?

I thought of the night before when I had tallied the bills and just when I thought it could get no worse; I remembered that the Ford was again at the dealership, Benji had totaled the pick-up truck and the house payment was due. There were just not enough hours in the day to do it all.

Wanting to be with my daughter on the soccer weekends was worth the angst I felt over my bills and not being able to make all my commitments. I knew too well what an adolescent girl traveling with coaches and fathers meant. I shuddered as I remembered the sense of obligation and guilt; the making-up for parents who could not be there and whispers of those parents who always were.

When I was Gemma's age, I felt that no price was too dear for a ride home or a hotel room, to save my parents the cost. I had become so good at separating my body from my soul that in the shadows of my darkest fears I wondered if these men felt ashamed of their power over a twelve year old girl, encrusted in a woman's body.

Now years later with fierce determination I would never let this happen to my daughters. I would never let submission mold their sexuality. I would never let sex rule their decisions. I would give them the strength of my trials, "Why go by foot when you can travel by carriage?" were the words that Charles Itten had written and I believed, proof my daughters would be safe. The trail had been cut. There was no reason my daughters or any daughters would have to feel the chill of cement on their naked back on a locker room floor. I would kill any man who came close to them and did not cherish them, as they were designed to be cherished.

Still, I unrolled the posters that had sat dormant in my closet since the truck had dropped off our Italian life 10 years before and handed them over to the shopkeeper. Garrett was a good man and his shop; *The Big Picture* did good things with their profits hence the name. He understood how a real life balance sheet was tallied.

He had opened the shop as a tribute to his father, lover of art and music, as a vehicle to fund

ಬ The Other Side of Tuscany ೞ

programs to help children have Art back in their lives. Had I not had Art in mine as a child I surely would not have survived. He and his mother fostered Art and its appreciation to all, especially the less fortunate. Its beauty spread like a warm blanket over their lives. Sad to think Art was not considered a necessity. Art heals all wounds.

Our mutual commerce would create light and programs and hope. This "investment" I hoped would one day be present on the balance sheet, though I never really expected any light back, except that in the bright eyes of the people, our deeds inspired.

A few years later, when Gemma told me she wanted to be a teacher or a coach I mused that the lesson had been well planted that day despite my afternoon tears. As she struggled to color an illustration for one of her projects and asked me to help her with a seed project for her second grade class she offered as if by script.

"I want to make a difference; I mean it is so hard when they are already older. They need an outlet, an inspiration- for some of them that is all they have."

I looked at her so proudly…

"Are you crying!?!" she said half incredulous, half teasing, I was. Blame menopause, blame lack of sleep, blame the Gattinara[1] whatever the reason, it

---

[1]Gattinara is a red wine with Denominazione di Origine Controllata e Garantita status produced from Nebbiolo grapes grown within the boundaries of the commune of Gattinara which is located in the hills in the north of the province of Vercelli, northwest of Novara in the Piedmont region. It was

was good to know my youngest daughter was not an accountant.

awarded DOC status in 1967 and received its DOCG classification in 1990.

Enjoy this moment in all its
fullness, and remember, you are
creating your life right now.

~Ralph Marston

Chapter 21: Sister's Grace

Apex, North Carolina, USA 2001

One year in a balmy November, "Le Grazie" as my
husband and his friends had affectionately dubbed
us after Antonio Canova's piece, assembled at my
home under the massive pecan tree. We were
celebrating a November Christmas in the garden as
the youngest, Sherry still lived in Dayton and was
visiting. With the occasion, we had planned a
shopping expedition with my daughters to an outlet
mall. We had done this with our mother when first
researching the various venues on the Eastern
seaboard for the American Adventure. The
daughters were delighted; the sons less so and were
getting a lesson in husbandry.

That day, I looked around at the circle at the various
types of chairs: Cane backed café bistro originals,
Chippendales, old Tuscan and early American. The
chairs fitting in their appearance to those of us that
sat upon them. The extravagance: expensive lawn
chairs and champagne luncheon: a true celebration
of ourselves in rustic elegance.

The brilliance of that afternoon not only in climate
but in mood, as the parcels were unwrapped with
relish, and squeals of delight and banter of the

bargains achieved with so little effort. How I loved my sisters and our children that day - confirming that even if much was lost in our American adventure - so much was also gained.

How wonderful, the ease of a holiday when the rules were re written by communion and not custom. Shopping was not my favorite pastime but it was a thread that tied my sisters to my daughters and had hemmed them together for a single Black Friday.

I watched as my sisters, now women, tumbled about with the children in the grass and slipped champagne from crystal flutes. All snacked on baked brie with raspberries and candied pecans on thick, crusty slices of Fresh baked bread. Life was near perfect had we had husbands. Or would it have made a difference?

I looked up to the branches thinking of that time on the bed in Linda's room and how I'd tried to be the big shot, the show off, the sophisticate and now, how I appreciated the humbling turn of events that brought us together, to savor our sisterhood. To savor family as only survival knows.

Addressing the branches above with gratitude and the reverence of prayer, I raised my glass to the setting sun:

> *When your life is shared with two*
> *countries, memories split between*
> *black and white, there are times that*
> *you feel closeness to your family in*
> *ways that are immeasurable and*
> *sacred, at times even forgotten.*
> *Thank you for these times.*

෪෨

After the tragic events of September eleventh, what seemed to be a lifetime career evaporated much like the towers themselves. As my job dissolved, my life bloomed with a confirmed truth that I had worth, despite how I felt on a daily basis.

My sisters had started their families. Young children are good at lighting the fire that keeps us going. Children will life into those too weary to fight to keep the candles burning. Children help us remember how important and perfect we are through their lack of judgment.

Europe had known what most Americans had stupidly ignored: terrorism can happen anywhere-even in America. As Americans, we hung flags and my children and I became strange again to our neighbors and our friends because we would not hang a flag in the rain or stop seeing our friends that were Hindu or Jewish or Muslim.

We prayed the craziness would stop. We prayed we would be able to fly again. The ocean seemed so wide now that the father of my children lived on the other side. We seemed so dangerously isolated to him now that America became a war-zone over night on the nightly news.

"Come home!" My husband's was the first call to come through as the second plane hit the second of the twin towers. Then all communication stopped and I wondered if God was trying to tell me I had made a terrible mistake. He was now sending me to hell.

115

I rocked at my desk as I waited to hear from Donovan or David. All silent. I prayed. Tell me, David is not on that plane.

David and I had been in London just a few nights before. I had flown in on the tenth, I was already in trouble. I had gone on my own for Labor Day. The deal was one that should have gone to Donovan and I could not understand why management was circumventing him. Some things you never know, but you do know, what to do for friends.

Donovan was in Japan and I knew that there were a lot of changes discussed behind closed doors. I had stolen my personnel file and saw the twisted mind games of the CEO printed and placed in my file. I knew I would be on the chopping block and really did not care. I had to protect Donovan. He had no idea. I had given all I could but I was worried about the naïve founder, who had become my dear friend.

David had left and went to work for an alliance partner after verbally whipping the management team in a conference call. He had warned me "watch out, you are too close to closing this and they will want to cut you out."

Holy Father, please. Keep him safe. Keep them safe.

I prayed the tears would stop. In horror, I watched over and over again the billowing skirt of the women and man clutched and jumping from the building. Symbolically, I felt David and I were doing the same.

For the three months after the attack, I would wake to screams and smoke and lay in a pool of blood. I felt I would bleed to death if I could not purge the grief I felt for the attack of 9/11 and my marriage that was exploding with the same unsuspecting terrorism.

C3EO

My family became closer to me and soon both my sisters would come to live in North Carolina. They nurtured my children while I globe trotted, being hired on the rebound by a competitor in Europe. Oblivious to the eroding forces within my life, I continued on the crest of my career like a circus performer on a tight rope. My children never sure what I did. My family never sure where I stood. My accountant never sure if I would be paid or when.

And I, surviving: paid bills, booked rooms, and hoped I would not die before shepherding my children out of a storm that they had no umbrella for.

To err is human to forgive is
divine.

~Alexander Pope

Chapter 22: Time to Move On

Apex, North Carolina, USA 2004

Three years passed. The children had finished high school and Kikka was in college. Still, my husband did not come. I had no time to follow what he was doing; I struggled every month. For Orazio, a man now in the springtime of a new courtship, my struggles were small potatoes.

I had started my masters because work was not as stable as I would have wished. They could never repossess my education and in times like these, sometimes that is the only wealth we can accumulate.

ഗ൭ഏ

I lay in the purple haze of dawn on Lake Johnson with a knot in my stomach.

My new love, Bud did not seem to want to be with me anymore. He blamed it on me- I was married and it was a sin to be with me. That was not it. There was something but I just could not place what it was. Later, I would find that this explosive, *sent from God himself* love story was just a week or 10 day fling for him. He had returned almost immediately to his old girlfriend using the excuse of me being married, as a shield to hide his double life. He wanted me to feel the wrath of God for cheating, a guilty adulteress, when in reality we both were, as was my husband for those of you counting at home.

I dressed quietly and searched for my cell phone. I would call my husband that morning and ask him for a divorce. I had wanted to do it for months but it was never the "right" time. At first my parents said not to spoil the twins' 18th birthday when he was to come that February. It was a perfect time.

It was getting harder and harder to make love to him. I knew but then didn't know, that he was with others, just from the things that he started to do differently. The questions he asked when we made love were not "his" words. They were the words of a lover. What if he made me sick… really sick then what would happen to my kids? Isn't that a good enough reason to be a right time? These are things your parents, no matter the age, will never understand. The right time: Is there ever a right time to tell the person you love and will always love, that you want him to just go away?

Divorce is not really what I wanted. I wanted the games to stop. I wanted the fog to lift and to know where it was that I stood, and where I was supposed to go. Instead, all I knew was that I was married to a man who lived half-way around the world, had a lover he introduced to his kids as his friend, and was destroying everything good about our shared history by listening to the edited version, compliments of said lover, devoted, fucking friend.

Yes, the best way to describe what I wanted was not divorce; I wanted him and all the accessories, lovers, rumors, and rewrite of my life- to go away.

"Pronto?" he answered half annoyed, half curious and I sat straight up, almost not aware that I had dialed the number and the moment had come, to let it all stop. I fumbled with a bit of small talk but he did not help me, in my discomfort. Now I realize he was probably with her. His answers cut me with their curtness. Had my daughter briefed him? Kikka had begged me to wait, again for the "right time, that time being while she was with him in Italy.

I hesitated and then began, "I think we need to move on... pack up our memories and get on with our lives...." then a song flashed into my head "keep the cat, take your sweater, we have nothing left to weather." A lump swelled in my throat and I did not think I could finish, much less ever speak again.

Bud came out on to the porch where I sat coiled on a stool, stroked my head and began kneading my shoulders. He frowned and swore under his breath when he felt the tension knotted there. He looked at my face it glistened in the morning sun with tears and though it was obvious I had been crying I was strangely pale. "Oh Pumpkin," Bud murmured sadly as he came out to the porch to see how the phone conversation was going.

"I want a divorce." This time I said it more convinced, but it was almost more for my audience than my husband.

"Is this what you want?" my husband asked

"Yes."

"Is there someone else?" he asked and I hesitated.

"Is there someone else?" he asked again.

"Yes, but he is not the reason. There is someone now in my life, but he is not the reason. This is something we should have done a long time ago."

"Do you love him?" My husband asked starting to lose his patience.

"That is not important. What is important is that you and I live the rest of our lives in some peace"

"Do you love him?" He asked me again.

"No, I love you, I will always love you but I cannot live like this anymore."

"Tell them, the children, you *have* to tell them. Write them a letter…"

"Is that what you think solves everything, makes sense of it all? It's not a letter, why can you not just talk to them – talk to me? Is that why you always wanted a letter from me, because you cannot deal with facing me, telling me that you just could not love me enough?"

My husband was silent. It would be later, as the layers of our marriage fell like onion skins on a kitchen floor that I would know the real reason for his distance. I left Bud's apartment and went for a long walk around Lake Johnson, tears rolling down my face and a pain so deep in my heart, it seemed all the vegetation around me would surely dry up as I passed.

In a couple of hours I would go back to Apex, post my assignment for the week, before the 12CST deadline and start the letter to our children. I really did not see the use of it; after all, they were not even speaking to me. No one was. I had felt solitude before and more often than not, welcomed it, but now my own breathing echoed, so empty was my world.

CʒƧꝋ

Dearest Benji, Gemma and Kikka,

I realize these past few months have been terrible and trying for you, more than I ever would have expected or imagined. In my quest to make things "right" I have made everything terribly wrong. The words of a Spanish song dance in my head from the CD Kikka loaned to me this summer, "Perdonami..." The CD had many songs, each that seemed written for your father and me.

Just as your father associates the Celentano songs to us, most love songs are not unique in their substance or their theme when you think of our Grande Amore.[1]

The love I had and have for your dad painful as it may seem, I can only wish that everyone can experience at least for a moment in their lifetime.

Fidelity is not a guarantee that love persists, nor is infidelity a sign that love has faded or died. In fact, adultery can even be a way -- albeit dysfunctional -- to try and stabilize a floundering relationship. In

---

[1] Big Love, a term used in Italian, for the greatest love of our life, usually the one we will always love not necessarily who we marry.

our case, ironic as it may seem, this is the linchpin to your father and I reestablishing our rapport. Everyone grows up in triangles, competing for our mother's attentions with our father and our siblings, and vice versa.

It is proven this teaches us to be terrified of abandonment and to resent sharing. It also causes us deep inside to doubt our worth in a relationship. To feel we are never good enough and will never live up to the expectations of our partner. This has been my reality with your father and his family and it has been an erosive force in our lives. Especially since, I was never the one he defended when I was criticized.

I never quite gave up on the childish fantasy that somehow, someday, I'd find someone all my own who only wanted me. But this is the destructive fantasy that keeps us looking for love in all the wrong places. I hope all of you will not make my same mistakes but learn from them.

Years of miscommunication and pride have brought your father and I to this point in our relationship that I am sure frustrate and confuse you. It is easy to say now "why did you not talk about this before" but I think both of us were afraid of what the discussion would be, secretly each hoping for some magical solution that would decide for both of us the outcome without having to deal with any confrontation or conflict.

In my mind, we were no longer married from the moment your father asked me for an annulment, (April 12, 1998) I felt he did not love me, and never had or why would he ask for such a thing? Your father on the other hand, had only asked for an annulment because he felt deceived and humiliated. So we merely put up with each other to protect you until the right moment came along so we could get on with our lives. I had hoped sooner rather than later, this moment would come.

I know in my mind I chased new ventures and technologies hoping for that "break" to fill a wheel barrel with money and go back to Italy, sweep dad off his feet and say "look, you do not need these people (his relatives in business) anymore". But that lucky break never came and as I chided your dad for letting others work him to death and take advantage of him, I allowed the same.

Unfortunately without the stronghold of financial backing that your father's family had, my errors were more costly and I have tried to repair them and continue to do so. Part of my lack of communication was the sad realization that I was not as successful as your father and did not want to hear the well-known "I told you so". And while my rewards are not measurable in money or houses, I still feel that the lessons have been valuable and to all of you in making you the great kids that you are.

Remember, you make a living by what you get but you make a life by what you give. I have given a lot and hope one day you will see the worth to this American exile.

The bottom line is that I needed your father and his help, it was very lonely trying to do this on my own but I wanted it to be right. I wanted for all of you the ownership of something that was ALL YOURS that no one could take from you. I was sick of the years of living in Italy and having nothing that I could call my own. Everyone seemed to have a piece of everything that your dad and I worked for and this was not right.

The sad thing is that your father never stuck up for me when I complained nor did he give me the security of knowing that I would be taken care of one day. I never wanted to discredit your father but I had years of anger and humiliation that accumulated from listening to all the "befanne gelose" I was tired and wanted to make sure I had something. I did not want to end up like your grandmother, Nonna Rina.

Twice your father had serious car accidents and I had a taste of what my life would be like if something should happen to him: I had the three of you, small and needy, with Nonna Rina, grown and needy, a restaurant to run, papers to be filed and no help just everyone complaining that Orazio should have taken care of things. What was frustrating is that Orazio was always taking care of things: for others. I decided I would take you to where I knew I had resources.

It saddens me to think this experience has been all in vain and you feel-all just for me. It saddens me to think in your minds I am just a selfish mother when I tried to be a mother, a mentor and an inspiration.

While I sit here in the kitchen a photo of Benji disapprovingly looks back at me. I have lied to him about his batman pants and I have been caught in the lie and now he stares at me in reproach. I imagine him in Boone doing much the same as he surely speaks to his sisters and dad. I deserve the reproach but I ask for your forgiveness.

I love you and have never stopped loving your father as bizarre and twisted as that may seem to you. What your father and I have is special and untouchable. I am sorry that my own needs and my quest to make it "right" turned out so wrong. I felt by announcing my relationship would somehow sanctify it into being more than it was, as the pressure mounted Bud was caught in a cross-fire that he never expected. The dog, the gym, the rest you all know - futile attempts at keeping me in his life when all was done. I tried to stay friends because that is my way... but it is not the right way with those that are weak and damaged, it just makes the wounds deeper.

Your father is willing to forgive and help restore what we have shelved for many years. He is willing to open a new chapter of communication, life and see whatever that may bring for the two of us in the golden of our lives together: But can you forgive adultery and lies and mistrust? Is there any sin that God would not forgive you of?

Remember, that we don't forgive because the other person is worthy. We forgive because we have been forgiven. Yes, there are difficult issues that you will need to work through and it will take time. Know that I love you and will always be here for you no matter your decision. Trust has been broken, you've been hurt by the betrayal, the deception..... But, those issues can be worked through, and it begins with forgiving.

You forgive the unfaithfulness. You forgive the betrayal and the breaking of trust. You forgive the deception... you need to forgive me and any other that comes to mind and hopefully we can overcome these things together. To err is human, to forgive is divine… I hope you find it in your heart to be in His image.

I love you and miss our conversations,

Mom

ೞ⊱

"What do you think?"

I finished reading the letter to David. It was almost a full minute before I realized he was no longer on the line.

My multitasking had taken me to the Hermes' website and I was playing with an animated line figure. In dragging the curser an orange ribbon would dance around whatever purchase you choose- be it a hand bag or a Private Jet - and form a graceful bow. I had not realized that so much time had passed and surely he was just livid, since this habit annoyed David when I had worked with him.

Whenever there was a conference call he spoke to me as if a small child, instructing me to put my head down on the desk so as not to be distracted and clicking about while on the call. At the time, my colleagues were all in the UK and I would be at my desk in Carolina.

He said my insidious clicking was a distraction and I would retort that it was their fantasizing that I was working in my underwear that was distracting them. I missed David and all the edgy fun from the gaming industry. We worked hard but played equally hard and somehow I felt he would not compromise and remain a friend.

It was days before I heard from him again. When I did it was in a terse e-mail.

David who had been there through the worse of it, who had called me every day, who had hired me after 9/11 when my world and the global community had been rocked to its core, retreated. His devotion had taught me that despite what I thought, I always had worth, even on the worst of days.

I had never been treated and pampered the way I was with him. The colors of friendship, devotion and respect played on the canvas in a way I did not think possible. If it was possible to have a playmate at forty with the simplicity one has at four, I had found that in David.

I was right. He would not compromise. It would be months later that we would speak. It would be years before we would return friends.

Love is an act of endless
forgiveness, a tender look which
becomes a habit

.~Peter Ustinov

Chapter 23: Crossed Lines

Apex, North Carolina, USA 2004

We were sitting in the kitchen. It was a beautiful
morning it reminded me of the beauty that had
captivated me and wooed me into buying the old
Victorian house surrounded by magnolias. The sun
had a golden glow and was coming in through the
sunroom next to the kitchen.

My husband, Orazio had flown in the night before.
We had so many plans of starting over again, I had
taken care to be at the airport on time and to bring
him roses. The dinner had been good even though
no one was really eating. Kikka had joined them as
a mediator.

We had opened an old bottle of wine, a Solaia[1] one
of the few left in a collection we had brought to
America from Italy. It was intended for all the
special occasions that we would have together but
never did. This was the first that we had opened
together yet it was one of the last few bottles in the
corner cabinet.

---

[1] Intensely fruity and complex with a good structure, well-
balanced, with soft tannins and a lingering finish. 75%
Cabernet Sauvignon, 5% Cabernet Franc, 20% Sangiovese
from our Neighbors, Villa Antinori.

Kikka had been mediating the situation for months.
She was about to finish college and had been
talking with her father almost every day. She
wanted to fix things, to fix our relationship, to purge
the girlfriend not that she disliked her, but rather
because she did not want anyone coming between
her and the things that were rightfully hers. She was
tired of everyone taking what her father had built
for them and that kept him away from his family.

Be it competition or care, he wanted to leave houses
and land to his children. This infuriated me as I had
witnessed the Corti clan's destruction by this very
thing. Greed wears many guises but when it is
draped in *family* the acrid taste can never be
removed from your mouth.

Kikka knew about Eleajora and yet I'd only recently
found out about her. I guessed, now that I knew
Kikka had known,, that she probably approved of
her father's lover while she condemning me for my
indiscretions,. Hadn't even Orazio's sister said that
this woman was "una donna eccezionale" an
exceptional woman? I wondered now if his sister
had ever said that about me.

We were sitting enjoying breakfast when the phone
rang. Kikka had left for school. I answered the
phone in the butler's pantry but the portable phones
made it impossible to hear clearly so I start to pace
looking for the right combination between
yesteryear home and technology to get through my
call.

Orazio automatically thinks I am leaving the room
so that he cannot hear the conversation. When you
have a guilty conscience, you always believe others

are guilty as well; he went upstairs to pick up the phone at the fax machine in my bedroom.

While I didn't know for sure if he was listening, I imagined he was.

Bud proceeded to tell me that he had checked himself into Dorothea Dix and that he regretted telling me that Katherine was the love of his life because I was "The best thing to ever happen to him."

I felt like I was hearing a sound track of a second rate film. Not Katherine he repeated. He hoped it wasn't too late, funny how competition sharpens priorities. The goodness in me wants to forgive him but mostly I want to just get off the phone, our conversation is only validating that I have made a huge mistake with my provisional freedom. The conversation is only making me realize what a poor judge of character that I am, as it is a repeat of a sound bite that earlier that summer he had retailed to Katherine.

He knew my husband was there. How did he, unless he was watching the house? I smelled danger, Bud was not well and the combination of him and my husband would be deadly.

Ok now I am "creeped out" and start to walk about to see if he is out in the yard somewhere. I am afraid now not knowing. What if he had a gun? Would he try to hurt us? A thousand newspaper headlines flash before me. I know what can happen; didn't Pacciani[2] start his killing spree with that first

---

[2] Pietro Pacciani was arrested as the "Monster of Florence", a serial killer who attacked and brutally killed seven couples

jealous encounter? And didn't he only get eight years because it was deemed a crime of the "heart," a lovers' spat? Where did Italians get away with reducing the value of a woman's life and that of her lover, to only eight years?

Holy shit, where is he? Half the time he was high and all the time, he is unstable. I am cajoling him. I'm telling him how much I care for him and that he needs to take care of himself. Of course, my husband is hearing this man tell me how much he loved me.

I was feeling sick and uncomfortable.

Bud said "I hope you're happy"

I said, "I am."

"Me too," came from the phone upstairs.

---

making love in the country side. The last victims were killed in our woods. http://www.monsterofflorence.co.uk/

Never waste jealousy on a real
man: it is the imaginary man that
supplants us all in the long run.

~George Bernard Shaw

Chapter 24: Danger

Apex, North Carolina, USA 2004

Even the best laid plans can dissolve when jealousy calls. Kikka was our greatest joy, turned terror over night with the arrival of the twins. Jealousy to blame, nothing else.

My husband came downstairs to me at the table. He came quickly and fast. He was smiling. I don't understand why he's smiling. Then his arm went back and he started hitting me. He started with a punch, and then opened his hand before he hit me. I think he realized that he was going to kill me if he hadn't. He was wailing on me. I did my best to cover myself but I knew I had to get out of the kitchen, it was too dangerous.

He called me a puttana[1], then screaming at me, "You tricked me. You had me come all this way, just so that you could trick me. You're still seeing him!"

He was crazed and angry and I was not fully registering what he was saying to me but mostly - WHY?

---

[1] Slang for "whore."

You have to understand, my husband can't hear very well. He doesn't speak English. All he could make out was that I was saying, "I can't talk now." And Bud saying he loved me.

In his mind," I can't talk now", means "my husband is on the phone". What I was saying was that, I didn't want to talk to him not now, but really not ever.

I tried to get out of my husband's way. The safest room in my house was my bedroom. I had a lock installed on the inside.

As I'm running into my room, haven't quite got the door shut, my husband comes in, instead of hitting, he grabs the fax phone, calls his girlfriend and says,

"My wife is a lot of things but I never thought she was a liar. And she has become a liar over this man. I'm coming home now."

Doing that, he might as well have ripped my heart out and stomped on it. I felt I could not move. I made no attempt to lock the door or get away. I just sat there on the bed shrouded in my sadness, again defeated by misunderstanding, his heart closed to a language that needed no words.

I just sat on the bed. I felt so empty. So desperate. I wanted to die. To melt into that mattress, just go away. As I was sitting there, he was standing in front of me, staring at me, my face red and swollen, my head held in my hands, looking up at him.

"I'm so sorry, so sorry; it is not what you think."

His hands clenched. I braced myself.

"There is nothing to explain, you tricked me you're a liar."

Later, he would tell me the whole time I was sitting there, he was thinking of picking up the aluminum bat and bludgeoning me. He didn't want to release me to this man. He felt in his gut that this man was using me. He would rather kill me than give me to someone who would not cherish me.

The phone rings. I suddenly remember I have a conference call that morning. I go to get the phone, but we struggle. Orazio thinks it is Bud again and he will not let me speak to him. The fax machine falls off my desk onto the floor. The phone unhooks itself. I'm trying to get the phone. Orazio is kicking it away from me. We're on the floor struggling to get the phone. The person on the other side is hearing the struggle.

When I finally answer. I hear, David from England laughing, "… Have you taken up juggling?"

While I never appreciated his humor, that lovely English accent is the sweetest sound. I was so grateful for the safety I felt hearing it now.

He is a dear friend. He will smell the rain and the approaching storm. Friends always do. David and I worked together at a company in the UK but rather than joke with him as I normally do, without moving my jaw to make what I will say is less understandable, I utter,

"Please help me, call the police."

"What?"

"Call the police", under my breath, so my husband couldn't quite make out what I was saying or read my lips, his true ears.

"Are you in danger?"

"Yes"

"Who is there with you?"

Click.

David gets off the phone. He would tell me later that blood was rushing to his face he had not met Bud but he knew that Bud had broken my heart. David had wanted me to leave my husband for years, especially after having to fly me out of Italy one year when I knew something odd was going on. It was when Beatrice had suddenly showed up and slapped my husband in the face on the curved street in front of our house. I had had an injured foot at the time and could not hobble down the 4 floors to go and see what the entire ruckus was about.

Italians are passionate about their food; maybe he had over cooked her pasta? At the time, I could only imagine that there was someone warming my bed. I had no solid proof. There were panties in the shower downstairs and soaps only women buy. I secretly prayed one day that it would happen and then I would be free but when it did, I was frightened and refused to believe this was part of my life.

I feared ending up in news footage in tiny pieces buried in the forest that bordered our home. I would not be the first of lovers to lose their life at Gli Scopeti. I had to leave. David was more than happy to oblige.

David frenzied, called the only person he knew in the area, Mary Flannigan. He had called her once before in the months after I had lost my job at LIPSinc. My daughter Gemma was fifteen and in the fear that I would lose yet another job when I became very ill thought to call David in the middle of the night while she and Kikka rushed me to the hospital. I had started hemorrhaging and delivering these pesky Fibroids. In hindsight it would have made a great scene in a horror flick the bloody, gelatinous masses coming down the heart pine stairs, as I struggle to breathe and keep from fainting.

Mary had been a social worker. Without any details she smelled blood. She proceeded to put everyone in place, she knew Bud was dangerous and she also knew Orazio was coming to town. Without any other knowledge she worked like a surgeon who doesn't know what she is up against, to save my life.

As fate would have it, living in that doughnut[2] where I live, they had to get the Sherriff involved, because Kikka during *the Bud thing*, had tried to get Bud and me arrested for adultery. They had a very long rap sheet at 101 North Main Street. They came in full force.

---

[2] The zoning term that designates an area as outskirts when in reality it is in the town limits. That said, the Sherriff must be involved not just local authorities, and he has the final say.

Police, sheriffs, fire department, ambulance. The whole front yard in front was full of emergency vehicles during the rush-hour morning commute.

My husband was having a monologue with me. What a horrible person I was. How everything everyone had ever said about me was true, that he never could see it. That I was "sensa anima" – without a soul.

"Exit now. Put your arms in the air. Exit now."

My husband looks out the window.

"The police are here..?"

Suddenly both terrified - we went downstairs.

Two police officers went in the house, after asking if there were any guns in the house.

"No." I wanted to tell him our arsenal was in the heart of Chianti.

They kept asking me if I wanted to press charges. The EMS person said they had to take me to the hospital. Mary was there, being Mary: perfect, composed, in control.

She called my brother in law Nick and told him I would not be coming into work that day.

He understood, and asked if Orazio needed bail money. Nick knew but mainly he had been there for me and my kids when no one else was.

"I can't."

"You don't have to"

"I just can't. It is all a terrible mistake"

At that point, Bud's mom, Carole came. Carole came because Bud called her after he had been on the phone.
"Mom I did something terribly wrong. I think Nancy's in danger."

She knew my husband was coming and that I was trying to make things right with him. She never wanted me to date her son. She knew how toxic he was: by-product of her own personal hell.

"Have your husband arrested. This is what you wanted," she said.

Her personal bad decision did not make it mine even if I had always thought it was what I wanted. There was something, something that left me there as if I were in the right place but just could not find the light switch. From our conversations in the darkest years of marriage with my husband, I had always said,

"I just wish he would hit me in America and then this would all be over."

But when he finally had hit me, I realized it couldn't end like this. It wasn't the way this was supposed to be.

Seeing him, sitting there on my porch with the police officers, hating me without knowing the truth was not the way. I just couldn't let him out of my life without setting the record straight.

One of us had to leave the house, if one wasn't going to be arrested. They pulled Kikka out of class to stay and guard her father – even though she was in exams. My sister comes around the corner after dropping her son off at school. She sees the circus that has assembled on the lawn.

Sherri bust into the house. She is relieved when she sees me and Orazio alive. She had imagined Bud had done something stupid.

"What are you doing? Stop this right now. Let him go!" She addresses the officers, this is what family does: they hide the pieces.

She's trying without knowing what had happened, trying to make it right, Italian style.

"We don't do this. We don't do this. Stop it."

 In family we do not fix things we hide them from view. If you ask Kikka, who came from Chapel Hill about that day she does not remember anything. Her and her father proceeded to rummage through all my things my jewelry, my letters my dried flowers from other men. Then they took it all removing any evidence that I was ever cherished by anyone. I was not deserving even of that.

Bud used to send me flowers for everyday of those three weeks we dated. I felt so loved and important. All the dried flowers they threw out. They purged the house of my sins. Then they took away anything that my husband had ever given me. They stripped me. It was almost like a bankruptcy. It was like the reorganization of a life, as if taking my possessions would humble me and break my evilness.

The Other Side of Tuscany

There's only one thing they forgot. One of the signature things that people always noticed about me. For twenty years I wore this thick gold chain, and hung from it was a golden slipper with a ruby. My kids used to love playing with it, they would turn it upside down and water from my shower that morning would spill out. It was like holy water dripping down my breast.

In their purging of my house, they took everything, everything, but this little slipper, this golden slipper slipped out of their hands onto the steps.

When I came home a few days later, I found it in the middle of the wooden steps that go up to my room. It was poised just like someone had run away and lost their slipper, as if a miniature foot had come down the steps leaving a magical moment.

I just sat on the porch in the sunshine with my friend after we left the hospital.

My sister did the best that she could, but we're Italian, we don't acknowledge, we just make it go away. We had to make a plan. Not for my life, but for Thanksgiving that was what was important, not my life, not my marriage, but a family photo.

We were all going to be together. The first time in 21 years we would all be together: Mom, Dad, John, Linda, Sherri, Nick, Linda's Kids, Sherri's son. Twins, Kikka, Orazio.

When the twins were babies and Kikka three, we took a family picture because my brother had cancer and they thought it would be the last chance to have a memento of all of us. We took that picture at

141

Christmas in 1986. I had gotten a black eye… my mother was furious,
"This is your last chance to all be in the picture together."

No one really wanted to do this picture, but it was so important for my Mom for all of us to be together. I remember combing my hair over the black eye just to make her happy.

In a way I was just doing the same thing again. Only this time the black eye represented twenty-five years of marriage.

We would all drive to Ohio together, but in separate cars. Orazio would have to be separated from me. We would tell my parents there that we would get a divorce. Parents were planning a graduation celebration for Kikka, and had invited all their friends for a party.

Before the party, the day of Thanksgiving, we told my dad and my mom what had happened. My father spent the whole day crying in this room. My mom ignored me, my sister-in-law and brother-in-law came to me and said, "we just want you to be happy. Don't pay any attention to your family, they just love Orazio."

I was on their side of the fence now the outsider that joins a family and is accepted but not welcome.

At graduation, my mom told two of my friends but other than that no one talked about the incident. To this day, I think my sisters glossed over this to my parents as if I had imagined it all.

"You just don't do this."

"Mom, let me explain this…"

"I don't want to hear it. You chose this bed, you lay in it. You left a career for this man."

At the party, my mom's friend Mary, and my godmother Mary, came up to me,

"Your friend Mary never should have gotten involved. She's not Italian what does she know?"

I said, "My friend Mary saved my life."

"That is not important. You know, divorce will kill your mother and father."

Then they walked away.

I felt like an actor on the stage going through the motions, I was completely hollow. My family was so much to me. In an instant, they had showed a different side, the one where honor is housed. What was so important was that everything be the way they wanted it to be, not the way that it was.

The way the family was treating me that even my husband was sorry. My husband, the day before we left, sat my kids down in the sunroom of my parent's house to say that he had been having an affair for three years.

"I don't love this woman, she's just convenience, but you don't need to be this bad to your mom. We all do this".

In that moment I saw compassion, saw him softening. He had been in for the kill the whole time.

"I hate you. I hate you I hate you." He was now, "you're not that bad a person. I've been bad too."

From that moment we left Ohio, until Christmas eve that year, I have no memory. Such was the pain of a horrific trauma to my entire being. My family had been amputated. I was hemorrhaging.

CʒƧ

I was so overwhelmed with nostalgia … I would be alone for Christmas. The kids were not even coming to the house. It was time to stop feeling sorry for myself and decorate the house.

I decided to buy a Christmas tree and a garland. I would decorate even though no one was coming. I went to one of my sisters' favorite gardening stores. It was more expensive than I where I would normally go. I was hoping I might run into my sister and see a familiar face.

Instead, I saw a man with compassionate blue eyes. I recognized him, but from where? I saw him looking my way as I struggled with the tree. Then he came over to help me.

He helped me tie the tree to the car, and asked, " How are you?"

"I'm doing OK, if I could just get the tree on my car..."

"No, I mean, How are YOU doing?"

As I looked at him this time, I recognized him: he was the EMS driver. I burst into tears.

"You're going to be alright," he said. And put his arms around to hold me. I breathed in the scent of the Christmas pine and his cologne, comforted. I wanted nothing more than to sleep in his arms.

Later, Orazio texted me. He was sending me a ticket. Come home. Let's talk.

"I STILL LOVE U." he had typed.

"ME 2," I texted my reply.

While the laughter of joy is in full
harmony with our deeper life, the
laughter of amusement should be
kept apart from it. The danger is
too great of thus learning to look at
solemn things in a spirit of
mockery, and to seek in them
opportunities for exercising wit.

~Lewis Carroll

Chapter 25: Face to Face

Gli Scopeti, Tuscany, Italy 2005

The nights never end, the sounds of the Greve
valley familiar and yet strange to me. I returned to
my house, not as a wife but as a visitor. Not as an
enemy but as a beggar looking for alms, crumbs of
a life I once had.

Why had he wanted to try? Maybe it was a trick?
He had a ski trip planned with his lover for the New
Years' week but did not go; instead he opted to fly
me over and "talk".

One thing was certain, despite all the pain and all
the hatred he had managed to stir up just for my
side of the equation, he was sorry. He had realized,
I did not deserve to have no one on my side. He had
come to my rescue when everyone else had
abandoned me.

Antoine had warned me, "Are you sure you will be
safe?"

"I am not sure, but I really do not care anymore."

The Other Side of Tuscany

It had been the longest Christmas of my life. I had no one to cook for, no one to buy for, and no one to kiss under the mistletoe. I had a tree, the first in years and fresh pine on the staircase. I wanted the house to be warm and beautiful in case someone would come by. It would probably be the Last Christmas here. I was hoping it would be my last on earth. Each breath I took ached with sorrow and I wondered if a heart actually broke when one lost a love so great.

We had been out looking at properties and there were clumps of mud and grass caked to the bottoms of my black leather heels with sexy zippers down the back. The phone rang in the restaurant and Orazio had told me not to answer, he did not want to open tonight. I hung my black mink jacket at the door and carried the cordless to him.

"It's Eleajora," I said as I handed the phone to him. He took the call openly. She had called almost every day since I arrived. I assumed she was still in the mountains since she had opted to go on the planned vacation alone.

He chatted for a long time in the restaurant and I returned not to see if he was still on the phone but to get a good bottle of wine. When he saw me he said to her, "Why don't you ask her?" and handed me the phone.

"Shit." I thought to myself. Haven't I talked enough to this woman? What could she possibly have to say to me other than - *Thanks for ruining our vacation.*

I thought to a monologue I had prepared for her after one of her calls when she assumed she had the upper hand. I could not ever tell her my observations as the discarded wife; such were her insults and her fury that day. My husband had angered her and she was getting even calling his wife.

She was a broken, mislead woman. Instead of feeling victorious I felt cheated and almost ally to her. Still, in as much as I wanted to help her, I wanted to hurt her because that was what she was doing that day. I was just too numb to feel, too disillusioned to care. I had thought to tell her that day:

"It is not that he cannot be faithful to me but that he is using you and you, without a crumb of pride, have succumbed to his every wish. Just as a prostitute fulfills what a husband dare not ask of his wife because he respects her, he has asked of you."

I had continued my mental manifesto:

"Do not be disillusioned, our sex life was fantastic. He had to teach you what I knew all along. I had to teach him how to enjoy certain pleasures... And by the way, I found your bag of trash in my bedroom's atrium I can dump it at your uncle's house on my way to Impruneta or throw it in the trash - or better yet, do you think your employer would enjoy seeing how you spend your spare time - especially the sex videos - real class - I'm impressed."

Eleajora spoke. "I really want to meet you I have heard so much about you and I think it is important that we meet."

She said it as if she were talking to one of the parents of her nursery school students.

148

The Other Side of Tuscany

"Really? I am flattered but I am only here for a very short while."

"Please, it is important," she continued.

"How soon can you be here? Have you eaten? We are home now and I do not know our plans for the rest of my stay or whether I will be staying. So if you want to meet, come here, now."

I looked at my husband whose eyes were now wide and he was mouthing to me that I was crazy. "Ma sei impazzita?" I guess I was. Why would I be concerned if she had eaten? I always equated sitting at a table as a gesture of peace; while I know this sounds crazy, peace is all I wanted.

I hung up the phone and then realized that I was alone and no one who might be able to help me, knew I was in Italy, except for my friends in the States.

What if *she* and my husband decided to get "rid of" me?

I dialed Antoine and told him of our conversation. I was frightened now. My husband told me he wanted to leave. I said, "No, I want you to stay."

Antoine told me to leave my phone engaged so that he could hear if I were in trouble. While I am sure made him feel better, I knew if there was trouble he would not be able to help me like Mary did.

In the background I could hear my husband singing.

149

Le notti non finiscono
all'alba nella via
le porto a casa insieme a me
ne faccio melodia
e poi mi trovo a scrivere
chilometri di lettere
sperando di vederti ancora qui.

The nights never end, and the
dawn brings a song to me,
accompanied by the closing of
doors on the street. Then, I
write kilometers of letters to
you, hoping to have you once
again, here with me.

The song brought me to my vacation memories with
my children; the words brought me to the painful
situation I was in.

Should I change? I looked at myself in the mirror
dressed in black from head to toe; my red lips the
only color I wore. No. I did not need to impress her.

She obviously wanted to impress me. Her "right
over" turned out to be over an hour. Her plans
revealed, as she sat on the couch a sexy, black lace
garter and no panties, probably included sex with
my husband after getting rid of his untimely guest. I
felt sorry for her. Is this all she saw of her now?

She walked into our home and kissed my husband
lightly on each cheek as if they were meeting for the
first time and she did the same to me as she
extended her hand for me to shake it. It was an odd
use of decorum considering the situation and a
Fellini film came to mind but I was having trouble
placing which one.

ເ⊃ The Other Side of Tuscany ⊂ອ

As she sat down and started her monologue I realized that she was shaking. I offered her a glass of wine and only hoped she knew wines other than this region. Earlier I had selected a Recioto della Valpolicella[1] one of my favorites from 1998 and it was a total waste, if she did not. Perfectly decanted, when she asked to smoke, I wanted to take the glass away from her.

Then I remembered the episode, Fellini pokes fun at intellectual pretension, but he also gives Steiner an important monologue:

Sometimes at night the darkness and silence weighs upon me. Peace frightens me; perhaps I fear it most of all. I feel it is only a facade hiding the face of hell. I think, 'What is in store for my children tomorrow?' 'The world will be wonderful', they say. But from whose viewpoint? If one phone call could announce the end of everything? We need to live in a state of suspended animation like a work of art, in a state of enchantment. We have to succeed in loving so greatly that we live outside of time, detached....detached.

Later in "La Dolce Vita," Steiner shoots his children and commits suicide.

I feel, as I listen to her, the same way I did watching the film, but there is no turning the channel or lowering the volume.

---

[1] Recioto Della Valpolicella is a sweet, unfortified Venetian wine DOC that was so named because only the ripest 'ears' ('rece' is Italian slang for ears 'orecchie') of each bunch of grapes were selected to make the wine.

She continues to talk and smoke in my house, albeit with her head in the flue of the fireplace, as my husband has instructed her. The lace truth poking out from her short avocado skirt, as she leans into the fireplace. It is comical but tragic. I cannot help but start to laugh at what is unfolding in front of me.

"Mica da ridere!" She scolds me, it is no laughing matter!

"You had a history with this man and now it is over."

She looks at my husband for reassurance but he looks away. She continues to tell me how much she actually loves him and how little I appreciated him or I would never have left.

I find no reason to correct her inaccuracies until she gives me the opportunity to show my husband that she is the source of the rumors that are circulating causing him embarrassment and discredit to our relationship.

"Your chance and the opportunity of others to sleep with him came because of my absence. Nothing more. I can accept that. I can accept your insults to my fidelity or homemaking because you have been tainted by what you want to believe.

"Since your lame opinion is of no importance to me nor is that of the little people you spread your lies to. I was a good wife. I was a good mother. I was an exceptional consort. To the people that matter: my children, my family and my true friends they know the truth. My husband, who at one time knew what was real and what was "chatter" will have to be re-educated.

The Other Side of Tuscany

"That is why I came back to him and put my own life on hold, until we set the record straight. Not so that he can liquidate you- he already has. You do not need a signature from me to get on with your lives- if he wanted you, he could have had you years ago.

Maybe you should look at public records instead of trusting sources that retail gossip with their withered lettuce so you will not notice.

I left my husband with everything

"Why do you spread these lies about me- they are lies are they not?"

Well, yes she agrees.

My husband looks at her and asks her specifically about one of the latest things she has told him.

She defends herself, "I am at war with this woman, no cost is too great." Then looking at me I see her hatred for me. I wonder how one can hate someone they do not even know. "I AM AT WAR WITH YOU." Ok, I get the point.

"No, you are wrong. The cost to my children is worth more than your stupid competition!" My husband is becoming more animated.

I am starting to not feel as numb, the soothing nectar of my crystal chalice now the right temperature.

"I did not lie about everything," she retorted. "Did you not always say that sex was a sport for men?"

She directs her question to me.

"Yes, I did say that and I believe it wholeheartedly. Just look at you, you are a perfect example of this..."

When she realized the insult she flung her glass at the stone mantle and started coming towards me. My husband restrained her and they started arguing. She was swatting him as if he were covered in flies.

Like a cat, I left the room and hurried to the front door. I could smell fear and the toxic scent that comes when an animal is losing a battle. I knew there were many guns in the house; I only hoped Eleajora did not. My husband was going to have to fend for himself, I was leaving.

Into the dark cloak of the Scopeti forest I ran. Once outside, the warmth of the wine could do nothing to protect me from the cold January night. So I ran faster across the bridge, towards the inn on the main road.

Once inside I wanted to crumble in the warmth of the woman behind the bar. I had no purse, no coat no passport. Tears were streaming down my face and I realized that these people must have thought I was crazy. My nose was bleeding again, damn high blood pressure.

"Who is chasing you? Do you need the police?" I looked at her wide eyed but the Italian would not come.

One of the men in the bar said, "Malia, when did you return?" I could not answer him and the woman hurried me to the rooms upstairs convinced that someone was chasing me and it would be safer than way.

Later my husband would learn that Eleajora had wanted to kill us both that night and had she a gun, would have. Her true colors exposed, my husband wanted more than ever to repair the damage and salvage what he could from a home that seemed on fire.

There is a set of rules when you are born into an Italian family. It is laden with loyalty and honor and trust. For each of these, there are special conditions that pertain to the men. There are exit clauses and excuses; annulment, even murder, is permitted when dealing with wives that do not know the rules. The women have more rules and fewer conditions. The Church makes all kinds of rules in Italy and lets you break them in exchange for confession and a monetary offering, or, in the cases of the women rape under a chapel veil. I just don't think they talk about it on the outside.

Amazingly, annulment is one the more honorable of the rules that allowing you out of the marriage, if you have the money. And ironically, allowing you to re-marry with honor in the church or without if not granted. Why did I not see that annulment means, "There is a new, good catholic woman in my life..." and not "I am erasing our history, our kids, your existence." I guess I could have been flattered when my husband asked for one on my 38th birthday.

Holy Father, why was I not given the rules of engagement for a Roman Catholic marriage?

All I wanted was a life free of bullshit and befane[2] like you.

What I cannot accept is that my husband who I always respected as being an honest and straightforward man, defender of the underdog, would belittle and destroy a woman who, I am told, is lovely and good.

What I cannot accept is that he betrayed you into thinking he would one day love, cherish and live with you. What I cannot accept is that he took away your pride and self respect to satisfy his selfish cock. What would people think if they saw the things I know about you and your depravities?

He destroyed you, a faithful friend and lover: companion and conspirer of dinners and delights, a maid to his unruly and unorthodox housekeeping. How was this possible?

If he is capable of this - who is this man I am married to and do I really want to be?

The line is so fine between love and hate. A simple word can change your life or end it. Instinct is more powerful than reason. When we lose ourselves to what is expected and what are good manners we forget what is safe.

Never let your guard down.

I should have known not to waste a good glass of wine on her.

---

[2] The ugly old maid that delivers gifts on the Epiphany it is an insult to woman who are petty and gossip especially of woman more beautiful than themselves.

Dreaming permits each and every
one of us to be quietly and safely
insane every night of our lives.

~William Dement

Chapter 26: Dream Summons

Apex, North Carolina, USA 2005

*Sitting down on the stone bench in front of the
house, I tied my running shoes. I could feel the
warmth of the grey-lavender pietra serena, serenity
stone, when translated literally, that had absorbed
the heat of the morning sun.*

"Damn!" I thought, "it is already late."

*I could not quite get into the routine of GMT + 1 as
when I was a child. Every night I went to sleep with
intentions of rising early, having a brisk walk or run
and then cuddling back into bed with my "Ori
bear" and a cup of steaming coffee well almost - my
hybrid beverage had the length of an American
coffee but the depth of espresso. It was no wonder I
had trouble sleeping, one time my sisters mused that
I drank the equivalent of 30 espressos a day. And
while they were exaggerating, I knew they were not
far from the truth.*

*Gemma my daughter now stood patiently before me
stretching her legs.*

"Come on Mom, you need to stretch too or you will never make it."

Never make it, she obviously did not know the competitive nature of her mom, and with that I make a silent vow to kick my daughter's presumptuous ass...but in all honesty, I know I would not even be attempting to run with my athletic offspring if she had not been recuperating from an ACL injury.

We start our run and the air is full of sweet, fresh scent of weaver's broom - the lemon yellow blooms warming in the late morning sun along the Strada in Chianti. We cross over the cobble stone bridge that connects their Tuscan home to the rest of the world and start towards the American Cemetery Memorial.

In a Twilight sort of reality, it is different - the smells and scents of Tuscany are there, so fresh and real but the scene is that of my home in the states, specifically Carolina. We are running in Raleigh but why, I wonder. A sick feeling overcomes me, I feel trapped and saddened.

This is wrong and I am suddenly overcome with dread and wanting to turn back but Gemma is too far ahead of me. I need to catch her before she crosses the second bridge. I am breathing hard my legs seem to be working in slow motion, I feel powerless. Still, I press on, salty sweat and yesterday's mascara; dripping into my eyes, my vision blurred. I feel like I am almost flying blind as I run towards my daughter.

I need to catch Gemma. Gemma seems to be letting me, as I slowly become more upright, my sneakers pounding the pavement in a flat-footed way. I have almost come to a stop when I reach Gemma.

Gemma was looking ahead. Just as I looked in her direction. I see a car barreling drunkenly towards us on the bridge.

Nowhere to move…

ଔ୫ୠ

I cannot move.

The pain is overwhelming.

There is water everywhere and I am looking through it. I cannot breathe… I struggle, I just want to sleep…I want to rest. I am tired … I am tired of running, competing. I just cannot do this anymore.

I close my eyes again but I can hear my daughter I cannot move to get to her - still - I can hear her. Gemma is sobbing and pleading for my help – GEMMA! Where is Gemma?

Oh my god, where is my daughter?

My eyes open. I AM looking through water. I can see the sun and the trees, a beautiful impressionist painting through the water…dreamlike and ironic, this period, my favorite, would pleasure me now in what feels like -my last moment of life.

I must sit up. I must. I'm under water, Yet it's so beautiful, so peaceful; the play of sunlight and tree leaves through the water lulls me.

*"Oh mmy God oh my God Mom.... My knee my legs
I cannot move them, help me MOM don't
MMMMOOOOOOOOOMMMM!"*

*Gemma finishes her lament almost in a scream. I try
to push my head above the surface, almost there but
my head slips under the water again. I open my
eyes. S someone is standing near me, a smiling face.
The woman is close. I can almost touch her; her
smiling face suspended slightly above mine, like a
Venetian mask.*

*I reach out to her and try to pull my head out of the
water again but instead can only look up at the
woman and hope she will follow my gaze to my
daughter and help her...I cannot resist the pain....*

CB8O

The telephone jolts me from my sleep. I am wet and
gasping, as if I was actually drowning.

My pillow is wet from sweat and tears. I am almost
tempted to not answer it but I am shaken and need
to tell someone my dream. Rinnnnnnnnnnnnnng
Rinnng Pause Rinnnnnnnnnnnnnng Rinnng Pause.

I untangle myself from the weaving of feather quilt
and linen to reach for the phone on my desk. I
answer, and then tumble backward into my bed.

"Pronto, Hello?" I answer in a deep, sultry voice-
my signature voice - not of someone just awakened,
but rather an asthmatic porn star- **definitely not** a
groggy wife.

In business, it had been my cold-calling fame - my
morning cold-calling that always warranted a return

call. At home, with phone stalkers and lonely hearts just calling to hear me answer only to hang up when I did not, that my voice had become a catalyst for a personal hell.

Assuming it was my husband I disarmingly waited for the reply but there was none - only hesitation.

I sat up, and again, "Hello? Orazio?"

"Disturbo?" [1]

Who the hell are you?

Was all that ran through my head as I tried to place the Italian woman's voice? **Then I remembered.**

Just as your body feels when jumping in to a pool in the dead of winter, my skin tingled and my blood seemed to stop flowing. It wasn't so much who she was -but what she was - that overwhelmed me. This woman was in my dream, now, out of the blue, she was calling me. Not even my dreams were off limits to his lovers!

I tried to catch my breath but the thoughts and the strangeness of it were rushing in so ferociously and all the possible reasons for this call were crowding out the logical ones. For a brief moment I imagined something terrible had happened to my husband…. But then in the next moment I was angered and cool….. *Why the hell was she calling me, if this were the case?*

"It's over, it really is this time." The woman continued in Italian. *What the fuck is over you crazy*

---

[1] "Am I disturbing you?"

*bitch? I thought to myself, there never was anything
to end .*

"He just left here and I am doing what he swore I
would never do because I am the type of person I
am, a good person, honest, beautiful..."

Wawa waaaat wat wat I felt I was listening to
Charlie Brown's teacher- well- Charlie Brown's
teacher in Italian.

Just add vowels to the end s of the Wa-waTs.

She continued her speech just as she did that night
in January in front of the fireplace in their
Florentine home. While she spoke clearly and
measured every word it just was not registering with
me.

"Just left here?"

Here as in *where*? How could he have just left *her
home*? It was mid afternoon in Tuscany, where was
our daughter Kikka?

Still listening, I get up and turns on the light-
"Bloody, non cosmopolitan fool!" I thought, there
should be a code of ethics for husbands' lovers and
what ought to be protocol, proper manners- when
calling wives. This woman did not even have the
decency to call until after I had my coffee.

Could she not do "time math" and understand?
Even our own children had learned to keep a double
internal clock from the time they were 5 and never
would have committed such a crime.

❧ The Other Side of Tuscany ❦

I cursed under breath searching for my cell phone as the "Waaat waaa" continued. I found it and quickly called my daughter's cell phone, "Siamo spiaciente, il numero[2] ......" replied the digital operator.

Then I called my husband's - busy. I wanted desperately to have confirmation that this woman was certifiably out of her mind. Unfortunately, no one seemed to be available to confirm this...so I resigned and listened.

My uneasiness turned to attentiveness, as I paced about the house half in angst, half curious and totally not believing the amazing dream and what it meant. Sigmund Freud would be having a field day on this one: *Husband's lover standing over drowning wife in dream. Dream ending with* said lover *waking said wife from it.*

It was an upsetting coincidence.... But I was listening...boy, was I listening.

"Si era qui a pranzo era andato al "Mulino"... He was here for lunch, he had been visiting "Mulino", You know the property "Mulino" right? The one he has been renovating for the past 2 years...." **"Of course.** " I lied coldly, stunned at what this woman was saying.

I had never even heard of this property we used to be in business together. Now we shared little but our grief; there had been a void over the last few years other than the random tidbits of news about the children. We offered and asked little, almost afraid of the pain that lurked in the shadow of honesty.

---

[2] "We're sorry the number you have called is out of range and cannot be reached at this time"

I really did not know what to do in a case like this. Wasn't I the problem solver, the "fixer"?

If you had a crisis didn't I always seem to have the magic wand to wave and fix it? Where was that wand anyway - I hadn't seen it in years?

I had never had a course on infidelity nor had ever been in this situation. Well, maybe once or twice when an insecure girlfriend or jealous wife would call and wake me after a business trip, fishing for details of a rendezvous or making accusations of romantic liaisons. I was often the participant of many of my co-workers' fantasies, working in an industry of predominantly post-adolescent males. And while I was in their dreams, I was not in their beds. The post tradeshow phone call responses were pretty much down to a science of being non-confrontational and painstakingly charming no matter how tired I was. Usually, the accuser ended up wanting to be my "best friend" and would invite me for drinks or dinner after profusely apologizing… all of which I would always artfully decline.

It's not that I was some sort of vixen…. even if my moniker in business was such - but I was the *only* woman, hence *other* was an adjective by default. Even so, that did not keep me clear of the wrath of gay lovers who also found pleasure in chiding me in the wee hours of morning after a show.

"We drank and were having such a good time- you know we have continued seeing each other since you left last time."

Jesus Christ, this woman should be in politics between her careful placement of a well-oiled script and the velocity of her delivery, I could not retort on one sentence. So I resigned to listening to romantic picnics and late lunches with wine that became entire afternoons together... and mostly, swallowing hard waiting for a moment to get even.

Then an unexpected twist in the fairy tale of *Me and Orazio* by Eleajora TheOtherWoman began the tale of *Poor Malia, Victim of Love.*

"Ok, now I know the bitch is nuts." I thought to myself... "she's probably sitting in my driveway holding a bleeding horse head.

"Who died and left you the position of Savior in my life? Vain as you are, get off your soap box and to the point of your call. I have not had ANY FRIGGIN COFFEE." I wanted to scream at her for babbling.

"I said to all my friends..." You have friends? I mused You manipulate people into thinking you are someone you are not- because of your own sad, interrupted life.
"If the bitch spoke English," I thought. "this phone call would actually have been an interesting conversation."

Resigned, I allowed her to finish her manifesto.

"I mean how could she live with this selfish, filthy bastard for 15 years??? Some mornings he doesn't even wash his face before going out...."

I continued my mental monologue since Eleajora did not even pause to breathe:

165

Excuse me, crazy lady where was that
Principe<prince> you mentioned in the beginning
of your call? I am having trouble following you.
Please slow down and pro-nun-ciate… Remember I
am a "Straniera", I can't understand if you keep
switching the story on me.
Remember we Americans are stupid and poorly
clad individuals, we are only good for sex and
breaking up marriages.

Back to switching the story, oh right, you are really
good at that. Yes, I still remember your words in
January: you are at war with me because this man
is the true love you have waited all your life for,
your soul mate.

Eleajora darling-sweet-little-Italian-perfect wife,
you are really confusing me now, when did you
realize you were waiting for someone else? On
Husband One or Husband Two of twenty-three
years? Yes, Eleajora, I am at war too. You may
have shagged my husband for the last three years
but your rumors screwed one of the most beautiful
love stories Italy has witnessed since Verona. You
ruined my reputation and rewrote my history not
only with the country I love but with my children.

I will get even; I will get my husband and justice…
just keep on talking.

We are recording now.

Forgiveness is the economy
of the heart…forgiveness
saves the expense of anger,
the cost of hatred, the waste
of spirits.

~Author Unknown

Chapter 27: Forgiveness

Dayton, Ohio, USA 2007

I look at the wall in front of me and see the quote looming," You have three choices Change, Adapt or Leave" What the wall doesn't say is just because you have three choices does not mean there is a solution in any of them. Nor does doing all three guarantee some result. Still I sit and I hope like I do most mornings when coffee and despair come to shake me from my slumber.
Why is it always a letter?

"You need to write a letter, you write good letters"
My mother was saying.

My husband had begged for a letter from me for years something to sanctify the years of our separation. Or was it something else? I was always the last to understand the sophistications of marital warfare. Maybe he needed written proof of some sort to get out of legal obligations to me and the kids? Maybe he needed something to share with his lover so that they could have a good laugh over my lack of proper Italian grammar and my unique language that followed me to Tuscany just as it had shadowed my life back in the states. When you arrive in a place where you do not belong you forge colony and communication with whom and what you know. Ours was a language of love and senses, textural phrases that took the fabric of my mother's sewing cabinet and folded it into the poetry of my father's pastry. We had big words from other worlds, flavors from countries and generations past and within the love of our family had woven it into a language all our own. This tapestry was my dowry to my children but outside of our family, it was little understood or appreciated.

My weekly letters to my parents were replaced by a Sunday Phone call. Partly because my mother says my handwriting had become a "Chicken Scratch" and partly because my mother says since I have become "Sue Sex a Full" my letters are full of big words she doesn't understand.

I love talking to my mother because there was a time where a weekly letter or a simple phone call was not so instantaneous and certainly not so simple. Not so long ago when I called my mom it was a luxury and could take quite a bit of planning. When living in Tuscany, I would have to arrange the call first by making an appointment in the noisy local bar. This public house that had the town's telephone before people had them in their homes was the only place to make a long distance call prior to cell phones without driving into Florence to the Posta Centrale. (Main Post Office)

The smoke filled bar filled with Italian men rearranging what I imagined a sweaty pork dagger in their pants while sipping wine and gawking was quite intimidating. I hated that I had to stand and

❧ The Other Side of Tuscany ❧

wait for the Signorina to call back that she had obtained the line with New York and would be calling me soon when my parents in Ohio were connected. As a non-smoker, the minutes seemed like hours hovering over these tables of men sitting playing briscola while I stood on display much like a prized livestock.

As a practical joker, some days I would melt into my private jokes, secrets that chagrined me when rumors would start. I did this by getting the best of these men that tormented me. I would delight in catching the glance of one and crossing my eyes and gesturing with my tongue so that he surely thought I was crazy and going to follow him into the latrine. Other times, I would cough without covering my mouth into whatever they were drinking to keep them on their toes and out of their dirty fantasy. Whenever someone moseyed up to me and tried to be desirable, I would ask them what was stuck in their tooth or hanging from their nose hairs in the loudest possible voice. If they were the first to speak- it was the usual,

"What's America, wantto fuck?" To which I would answer in perfect Fiorentino, "I would but your boyfriend gave me syphilis."

The bar usually quieted down after that and I always imagined the "hard-ons" did too.

Sometimes people would laugh, but mostly they were unsure about me.

If my mother only knew - what I had to endure to call and talk to her? Then again, she probably would have scolded me for being cheeky with these men who "meant me no harm".

169

All men mean you harm when they are in packs, the hunter emerges and logic retreats. I know this, my mother doesn't and I thank God for that.

Whenever there was a soccer match on television I could enjoy a Flute of Prosecco[1] relatively unscathed from the crowds as not even the "Fica[2]" can distract an Italian man from soccer.

Today I luxuriate in speaking to my mother as my minutes are free and so is my mother, knowing no money will be wasted on the call. She gleefully goes through the obituaries since I do not get the Dayton Daily News. Somehow she cannot understand why I would read a newspaper from New York if I never lived there and not read the Dayton Daily News. She then continues on to Ann Landers and there is always "a lille piss of paper" that she has cut out earlier to read to me but now cannot find, so she will mail it in a letter.
Then just as I think I am going to get off the hook she brings up Oprah.

"Did you see Oprah?"

"Mom, I told you I don't watch Television."

Even though I must have told my mother one thousand times that I don't watch Oprah the phone conversation always goes there and somehow it leaves me with this sick guilty feeling that no matter what I do, I have done my mother "un torte", a sin by having an Oprah–free lifestyle.

---

[1] A Sparkling white wine from the Veneto region, used as an inexpensive substitute for a champagne cocktail.
[2] Vulgar term in slang for a woman.

The Other Side of Tuscany

We have an expression in Italy, "Few but good" is the translation. I did not watch many episodes but the few were good.

It was in Ben's room, the only room with a television, that I watched the show. The couple sat on the couch, the husband sheepishly looking at Oprah and his wife, as he calmly and methodically reported on his infidelity and how she was oblivious to this obvious fact. To many around her, even her sons knew the truth, she was not only betrayed by the actual act but the ruse that was their "perfect marriage." Sadly, in the perfect of couple and the cherishing of a devoted husband and father were hidden the secrets of many relationships over many years.

Stunned. I sat there. Stunned I wanted to get on a plane and be this woman's best friend. I wanted to hug her, open up a perfectly aged wine and make her something to eat. I was not the only one.

She looked great. She looked like she loved herself and him for that matter. Then the son came on and though he was an adult probably early thirties, he looked like he was ok, a success, he loved them both and when he hugged his dad they started to cry and so did I.

I did not want to rush out and hit the man, I wanted to understand. I sat there in my son's room for a long time after the program finished. I knew I had to speak to this woman. Forgiveness she said was the greatest gift we could give to each other. Rekindling love among the ashes of infidelity was worth a try, especially if it meant finding ourselves.

I continue my letter with resolve to work on my road back and to watch more often.

I start and stop again. The letter to my husband, the book, the letter to Oprah but now maybe there is reason to finish.

The reasons are always different and in some ways always the same. I need to write this book. Mainly, I need to have a project or I may not bother getting up any more.

This book has been my project and while I do it for me to heal, I do it for you, the reader to deliver you from your own hell. I know how it feels to be so deep in hell, the only relief you have is to think that one day it will end.

If you are lucky, you have family or friends and live for their milestones, having giving up on your own and simply going through the motions of life because you can breathe. Even then, you have to sometime remind yourself to do so.

I have never been in the story book, fortunate love story. I have always been the Greek tragedy or rather Italian one. The kind where you can smell the danger and see the sleeping heroine but you choose suicide anyway, knowing you will never be "happily ever after".

So why after 25 years of drama is this one is not temporary? What did I do to deserve all this?

A suffering so long and hard and intense that it came from the generation before me and like a hurricane gathered force and spun into the generation after me. I think none of them will ever be able to love with intensity and abandon, from the pain I have inflicted.

Dear Oprah,

So here I sit starting my 1000th thought to a woman I do not even know but who sometime during my European life took the place of Phil Donohue and Mrs. Wilcox to become the new spiritual guide of my family.

I do not even know what I want from you other than a chance to have you listen to my story. Maybe then, it won't seem so bad, maybe then, it can morph into someone else's life and release me from my own. Maybe a critic will come back a year later and tell us all that it is not true it was all a bad dream and I never left Tuscany. I deserve to be free from all this, my family deserves to be free from all this: the secrets, the lies, and the deception.

I don't even know you, yet here I sit. I have only seen your show in snippets after being called by my mother. I did see a whole episode once and maybe that is why I sit here today scribe to a train wreck that was supposed to be "until death do us part." It was probably in the darkest hour.

Although from a poetic sense, I am embarrassed to write that in my darkest hour, I found the remote control of my son's television set so that I could watch a taped show.

I had always liked watching the news and would religiously wake my children every morning from the time they were old enough to comprehend English to watch Dan Rather. It would be 530 Am

GMT+1 but it was direct from somewhere in America. Years later, the children would comment that they thought he was the president of the United States such was the ceremony I held over watching the show and the reverence that followed after Mr. Rather disappeared from the screen.

I tell them they owe their English to him.

Your show had been on earlier that week and my sister and even a friend commented that I should watch it. "Back from something" was the book that this woman had written. They both had said, "this woman is going through what you are but she came back from it."

Come back from what? Hell? I wondered at the time. So what, if the "coming back" leaves you so damaged and humiliated, why bother? Then again, I ached so much that anything was worth a try and certainly, watching Oprah was not nearly as messy as putting a gun to my head.

So I watched it. Your show of a woman, Suzy Farbman who had always thought she was not growing in the relationship with her husband. She felt that somehow there was something missing when it felt like they had it all. They had done so much together, grew their lives and careers; and had it all, yet they were empty despite the great love and respect they had for each other.

Suzy had written a book and when she held it up I understood, "Back from Betrayal. Saving a Marriage, a Family, a Life."

Oprah, maybe you could help me find her, connect and find my way back?

Warmest regards,

Nac

ᘯᘰ

The half truths are really half lies, that are hiding a truth so terrible, you would opt for the lie any day. Even now, I will not disclose you the names of boys, now men, the men now old, the liars and cheaters who are not strangers to most of us. Though I have thought about it and some days, know I would not have to suffer as much if they atoned for what they did.

Forgiveness is the greatest gift we can give to each other.

Here, I offer it now take it; I have given them everything else.

I fear one day I'll meet God, he'll
sneeze and I won't know what to
say.

~Ronnie Shakes

Chapter 28: What's in a Letter

Apex, North Carolina, USA 2004

Our father, who art in heaven, find it in your humor and your heart - to release mine.

I try each day to get through to the end and some days, no longer appreciate the gifts you have given me, much less remember what they are. Forgive me.

I live because, I love my children but even they know not their mother, only her sins. Forgive them; they know not what they do.

Release my heart from the coffers that contain it and from the man that I no longer know. If I cannot have him here with me and my children, make him happy and keep him safe but let me come and get my things -safely.

And please God, give me good health and a bad memory so that I may live out the rest of my life without the torment of Tuscany but copious amounts of Chianti.

Amen.

Sister Mary Francis would have had me kneeling in the back of the church, dried beans under my knees and two Webster unabridged dictionaries on each uplifted-to the- heavens arm asking for forgiveness had she known the content of my daily correspondence to God.

Still I pray. God has a sense of humor which is why he gave nuns big hairy moles on the parts of them that you can see and not the skin concealed under their habits. That is why, when my husband told me that he no longer wanted children, I was blessed with twins. That is why; he gave my mother diabetes so that she could appreciate my father's baked goods before she left this earth, as she never liked sweets before. His humor is true as the furry freckle on Sister Mary Francis' neck.

I have proof in God in his grace and in his humor. I have my prayers and my rites. I have religion; I have a church whose cathedral ceiling is made of branches from the mighty oaks of Raleigh and the Cypress trees of Tuscany. I do not follow rules, I am Catholic, I am Buddhist, and I am curious. Yet the lack of conformity makes me unholy and this is terribly wrong.

"Nancy, write me a letter."

This was my husband's daily prayer.

Many of us no longer have the culture of hand written correspondence, but I always did. While I set whole days aside for letter writing, this one letter dried all writing, all imagination and all humor, it even silenced the prayers. Prayers and holiness had now been placed in the box with the summer of my infidelity. In all the craziness that comes with passionately breaking vows, ironically, it led me back to God.

Many of our children will never know the joy of a hand written note in the midst of summer from a classmate. Yet I remember my friend Celeste and I buying our first stationary: mine was bright Orange with sunflowers and 1960ish doodles, hers was cool and pale in contrast. Still, even the buying of pretty paper and a new pen, the letter to my husband did not come. What did he want me to say? Was this the wax to seal my fate - only a ruse he and Kikka thought up to kick me out of their lives? Were my questions only more excuses for not writing a letter that could appease him?

Sometimes, this book feels like a Postal Secret[1] to Frank Warren (only longer) but the relief of revealing never comes, as all the secrets never come. My first secret would be: "Many see to give away their first born a sacrifice, yet I would gladly." Especially, in the first years she arrived in America when I no longer felt welcome in my own home.

The home, the twins and I cherished was seen as old, impractical and not right for someone *like me.* Who was *me,* in the eyes of this daughter that as a small child told everyone I was dead and *Nancy* was a friend to her father. Sadly, Kikka's disapproval let doors slam breaking delicate Venetian chandeliers

---

[1] Post secret: Frank Warren created the website on <u>January 1, 2005</u>, Post Secret has collected and displayed upwards of 2,500 original pieces of art from people across the <u>United States</u> and around the world. The site, which started as an experimental <u>Bloodspot</u> and is updated every Sunday with approximately 20 new pieces, has a relatively constant style, giving all "artists" who participate some guidelines on how their secrets should be represented

and stained glass, and stomping feet battered tired heart, pine floors. She damned our home into an impractical shelter for her odd mother in a strange land.

Not because I do not love her, but I harbor the resentment of a mother that is betrayed by her child to her husband. I feel betrayed by a child that not only knows her father's lover, but compliments her and converses with her. I feel betrayed by a child that does not harbor ill for a man that has done for another's child more than he has done for her, yet at every opportunity tries to bite the hand feeding and protecting her. Then again, that is not the only secret and this is typical of teenagers. Terrible as it is this angry thought, on the cusp of police at my door, I love her.

We have had a love and hate relationship since the womb and maybe it is for that reason it has played out to be like this? I started it by keeping a diary when I was pregnant with her. Maybe that was a mistake. No the mistake was on her 21st birthday I found it and gave it to her. I was heart -broken when I learned of my brother's cancer and my pregnancy with Kikka was so precarious, I had been forbidden to travel to be by his side.

"I do not know you but he has been my light and my champion for 25 years. I cannot lose him. I cannot say good-bye without trying to will life to him as he had to me, that January so many years ago. Forgive me, please understand little stranger growing in me"

On my post card, I see the swatches of fabric from Pucci and the bright colored swatches of chintz from my own company, the hand written menus with swirling calligraphy and the "picture letters"[2] to my children adorning my "post card" that holds the terrible secret that no one knows. I see my husband, I see him seething with jealousy thinking of me in the arms of another man but yet no fault that he is in the arms and life of another woman. He has told me there have been many. And while I want to know - I don't.

The problem is which terrible secret should it be? If it comes to the light will it dry up and finally go away? Or will it harden like a starfish, a souvenir on the dresser, painful reminder of a life taken just to have it on display?

Take a letter Maria, sent it to my wife....
I am gonna stat a new Life
Last night, as I got home, about a half past ten
There was the woman I thought I knew in the arms of another man.
I packed some clothes and I walked out...and I aint goin' back again.
So take a letter Maria...address it to my wife
Say I won't be coming home...gotta start a new life
Oh Take a letter Maria, address it to my wife
Send a copy to my lawyer...gotta start a new life

I remember the melancholy, the despair as Tom Jones[3] sang out this ballad to a women he loved

---

[2] When the children were small and would spend entire summers in America, I would write to them in letters composed of childlike hieroglyphics since they were too small to read.
[3] Popular singer in the 70s.

now in the arms of another man. In my "youngness," I only saw his letter. Later as a woman scorned, I saw his true motive, it swelled before me in his tight gabardine pants gyrating and taunting the audience. He just needed something in writing before he took his secretary out. It was right there in the last line of his song.

It just so happens I'm free tonight, would you like to have dinner with me?

I have memories sitting on the couch with my mother awaiting Tony Bennett on *The Tonight Show* only to have Tom Jones. Fondly, I had remembered the glee on my mother's face, confirming Tom Jones was not bad either as we sorted clothes late at night. The song now mocked me taking all that was holy from the late night ritual of my mother and me pairing socks with Johnny Carson.

My husband has taken of late to sending me songs. Could it be that in Music there is healing, could it be that they have the words that lay dried in our ink wells? If I were to credit Oprah and Suzy for inspiring me to reconcile I am sure that he would credit Celentano and Ramazzotti for his inspiration. Divorce Italian style, American journey joined together by a simple request, "put it in a letter."

When we were younger I would write him every day even though we lived in the same house, it was easier for me to express on paper what I wanted to say to him. The words flowed and I could correct what my ears had heard.

"Language" is my own; processed and stored in a way unique to me and my family. A word from

181

home, one from the old country, another from the bowels of a ship that brought them to this new land. The meanings not correct but sounds so pleasant, they were used often and incorrectly. Our communication was one of rhythm and food and like the later, consumed with pleasure and abandon, without rules.

The patrons at the bakery could listen to my father for hours. I had his gift. In a real world, or better, that of "the busy people", no one collects a language as such. So when I learned a colorful expression from the fruit vendor, I knew best to check if "Porca Madonna"[4] was in the dictionary before I used it on my husband describing the day's events. Another was, "Viva La Figa[5]" unacceptable for a lady to be singing, despite how catchy the tune.

I would check and make sure I had the right word, allow my calligraphy to wrap around him like my legs had earlier in the day begging him not to leave and go to work. Now, it was difficult knowing that someone else's were wrapped over his waist and that I had been in the arms of another. Yet, I craved that thread that we had, ever so delicate when he would return from work and look about the house then showered and changed for dinner. There was always something new and a letter. Now those letters carefully tied with ribbons and bows lay opened in a field or fireplace ash. How dare she touch my writer's place, rummage through the drawers that contained my dreams, my journals, and my letters to my husband? Was it just to leave me one of hers?

---

[4] A blaspheme used among Tuscans.
[5] A crude drinking song of "long live the vagina."

The Other Side of Tuscany

Her letter has voided me and my words, just as the impatient English teacher had years before when I said I wanted to be a writer.

CR&O

When Gian's cancer came and back I journeyed back to America to care for him with Kikka and twins in tow. I would ask Orazio those five months,

"Won't you write to me sometime?"

His answer was always the same, he did not have time. When he finally did write me, we had drifted so far apart; the distance did not allow me to comprehend his words, almost, as if I was actually reading them from the distance where I now lived in the states.

How many letters would be written to perfect strangers pouring out my heart? They were easy and intimate. Easier to tell a stranger how much I loved my husband, harder still for them to understand, why I bothered.

When the request fell upon my shoulders from my husband the ink dried in my mind and never touched a page. There is something ill-omened of a letter that is written and re-written in your mind a million times, that when you are told to write it, evaporates. There is a quality in the love letter when love is being borrowed. It is lost between the shores of an ocean and has the hollowness of a last minute college assignment, when demanded. Then there are the words that come to you in the melody of another. That tug on the chords of your heart so tightly that you know the song was written for you because you have been thrashed to your nakedness

183

such is the pain of true love. Celentano knew the words to our letter when he wrote, "L'emozione non ha voce,"[6] emotion has no voice.

Just knowing we were not alone in our void, gave the reassurance my husband needed to look past the crumbling walls. He walked around the ruble of our marriage and searched for the strong box to carry out into the light.

---

[6] The song in its entirety is at the end of this book.

Jealousy is no more than feeling
alone against smiling enemies.

~Elizabeth Bowen

Chapter 29: Lust

Gli Scopeti, Tuscany, Italy 2005

The ironic thing is that I lay here and wonder with
that sick feeling in my stomach, about their
lovemaking. If it was as passionate as ours or as
loving or if I am merely delusional in thinking that
our sessions were so wonderful. I was really getting
lazy the last few years. I was really hoping he
would not like being with me anymore so that he
would just leave me alone. I silently hoped he
would meet someone but never had I dreamed my
wishes were so true. Not because he repulsed me or
I did not feel the need to a good seeing to, but for
the simple fact that when he left, I craved him. The
craving for the first few weeks after he left would
make it impossible to function without having a
session or two on my own before I would start my
day.

Did they spend hours ridiculing my passion that
seemed to make men spellbound? They were
spellbound alright, but it was more than the sex, it
was a delicate weave of contrasts: the young yet
worldly, the stranger who made you feel instant
confidence.

Emilio had told me the enchantment lay in my fiery
eyes. The eyes that laughed and the smile that

185

danced, made anyone who met me instantly like me and do whatever I wished, well at least for a while.

I think back to the years when my children were small and my father was concerned with the sudden disappearance of life from my letters and came to Italy to investigate my well-being. To his dismay he found his stoic eldest daughter, the glue of the family, hardly keeping herself together.

"You know I don't mind that you live half way across the world nor do I mind you are practically not an American anymore, but I do mind that you do not smile anymore."

I looked down to hide the smile that was forming on my lips. I was convinced he was going to say something about the way I was dressed. I had lost so much weight. Lately I could hardly keep anything down so strong was the urge to vomit every time I had those feelings of in adequacy.

My husband seemed to reveal in the fear I had in not being what everyone expected and in making sure I had nothing decent to wear that might show off my figure. I wore old outfits of his clothes fashioned into feminine things for me. At first I altered fervently and then I just did not care; the more my body was hidden the less trouble I was in if someone looked at me.

I would have Augustino make little shoes for me; the wonderfully crafted Italian men's wing tips were my wings. They could take away everything from me, rob and wear my spirit, but I would always keep a spark.

The shoes were the symbol of my spark. Even when they would cut off my hair, I stared down at my shoes and they caught my tears. As they bounced from the soft kid hide I swear I saw diamonds and fairy dust. I knew I would make it. I would not dim.

"And, I think we need to get you some clothes." My cheeks flushed and I could feel a knot form in my throat when I looked at my father as he choked on his words and fought back tears. He had seen more than just a daughter whose letters had gone dry; he had seen a young maverick's broken spirit.

As I looked back on that time years later, I was amused that the sadness and shame of that afternoon had been replaced, almost like a life not my own but a sample to observe; like seeing a Fellini Film with intellectual observation, no emotion just a slide or two from the "dolce vita" retrieved from the cutting room floor.

CRSO

The hardest thing for me to accept is not my husband's criticism but the comparison that is implied. When he tells me that I am not perfect, he only reminds me that his lover was, at least in appearance. "L'unico defetto e' che ha un culo un po piu piatto" (The only defect was a flat ass.) Too perfect; you always said that together the two of you obviously did not match.

Need I remind you that I do not now have, nor have I ever had, parents catering to my every whim or any extra money to spend on "me." – I always have and still have to take care of everyone else before I can even imagine thinking of myself - much less something as superficial as my appearance?

Need I remind you, when I was beautiful it was a problem. You never told me and when others did – it was so easy to fall out of love with your lack of attentions. So it was easy to fall in the web designed to catch my weakness and to fall for the men who told me that I was. You never appreciated or told me that I had any worth. It is no wonder that when someone finally did see my value and constantly told me, I was star struck.

The love and sacrifice I have made for you. Why do you continue to fall back into where you were which is the very reason I left you in the first place. You are not deserving of me. It is no wonder you are alone - but why do I have to pay for your sins?

It's important the people should
know what you stand for. It's
equally important that they know
what you won't stand for.

~Mary H. Waldrip

Chapter 30: Cleansing

Gli Scopeti, Tuscany, Italy 2005

Cleaning was therapeutic. The cleansing of a home
and the secrets it contained was a chaste ritual to my
own cleansing. It chased my sins, the ones I never
acknowledge, the secret, carnal indiscretions. Now I
was cleansing his from our home.

It was my only release, the only finding of a woman
left behind so long ago. Sometimes I caught a
glimpse in the mirror and wondered if others saw
me that way or how my children did as a loser? Or
as I now felt coming home, like a Cinderella of
sorts.

"That woman", the irresistible spell as I was once
described, had drifted in and out of my married life.
There were reminders every time I walked through
the Piazza della Republica or by Raspini.[1] Everyone
knew "her" or "of her". It had baffled the Gandolfi
girls that months before I had come to live with
them people that people were calling for "her".

---

[1] Iconic venues in the center of Florence, where people gather
to see who is new in town.

I was young and beautiful then yet I was not like the others, I was kind. I made time for everyone I encountered. Each day was a mission to spread joy even if my own heart was wallowing in sadness. Any man who ever asked me out always warranted a first date, no matter his looks, his wealth or his origin if he was polite and gutsy enough to ask I would go out with him. The models and other designers thought I was mad. "He is a student for Christ's sake still living with mamma, and look at his ugly shoes!" They would chide me. I cared little because I knew better than most, where real beauty lay.

03&0

My eyes stopped scanning the multi-colored plastic bottles and actually started seeing them. They stopped on the bottle of Drano, as I pulled it out of the cabinet I remembered something horrible my friend Regina told me years before.

I put the bottle back as if the very idea would harm me.

What could have upset Mrs. Applebaum so terribly that she drank Drano and died an agonizing death on the bathroom floor?

I remembered what my best friend Regina had told me that morning at the bus stop when they were in the ninth grade. Though Regina was not one to fib or exaggerate, I had secretly wished that she had. The death of their neighbor, eaten away by the chemical cocktail designed to clean your toilet was violent in its truth and in the symbolism.

The Other Side of Tuscany

Did Mrs. Applebaum feel she deserved so little respect even in her suicide? Then I remembered Mrs. Applebaum's children a boy and a girl much younger than myself at the time. I closed my eyes to see them and could not. I whispered a prayer for them and their mother. May they all have the peace they deserve, but somehow that seemed impossible. How could they? Coming home from school and finding their mother retching and bleeding on the bathroom floor. My own mother had dropped some Drano while cleaning the master bathroom at home and for years afterward, there was a bleached bald reminder on the avocado sculpted carpet.

CB80

"Certainly, after all she did to you the only logical reason to go back to her would be to save the family, right?"

My husband was quoting his aunt's cousin who was the original match matcher for my husband and his most recent lover, Eleajora.

Eleajora had to save face in the town and since for family we do everything, it was a good enough excuse. At first, she had told everyone that the only reason my husband was not marrying her, was because I was holding the deed on the house and control on bank accounts (or some other fib he had invented to not commit to formalizing their relationship.)

Now she had to deal with me returning and not leaving causing not only an interruption to their "love story" but a real kink in the story she was circulating on their future together.

With that comment, like many of the cruel stabs poked my way over the years, I felt the acid in my stomach start to churn.

My instinct made me want to hurl the plates I was clearing to the patio floor, but my love for the Vietri[2] painted plates with bright colors and happy animals, stopped me, so I simply rose from my chair. Torn between controlling myself and the image of Eleajora dumping a skillet of Spaghetti on his head, I started erupting into a manifesto of my feelings for small minded people. No words were spared for his former lover. No words were spared for the false friends and the townsmen of Impruneta.

"What *I did* to you?!?" I screamed, "how the hell does anyone know what I did - OUR history, and why the hell do they care? Why was it so important to dissect every detail of our lives and rewrite history and retail it over and over!?!"

"They know, they know. Everyone in town talked about us….you…we were a 'favola'." [3]

"Bullshit. That is what you and your precious whore would like to believe. No one talked about us in the fervor she would like to think. People admired and envied you and a lot of that was me. I was an easy creature: always happy, always smiling - it was refreshing to see that after the all the whiney, diva bitches you always seemed to find. People who genuinely cared about you, were pleased for you and those who were not, pissed in your well. Had they not, you would have come to America with me

---

[2] Brightly colored ceramics with naïf animal designs from the Amalfi coast.
[3] A fairytale.

The Other Side of Tuscany

and all this would never have happened. You let your own insecurities and their chatter rob us of nine years of our life. Are you going to continue to do that?"

When would it ever stop I wondered? I ran inside to get my tennis shoes, my vision blurred with the angry tears that now streamed down my burning cheeks. It seemed as if the blood in my head would start pouring from my ears the pumping was so loud. I knew my blood pressure was rising and if I did not get away, I would probably have a stroke.

He usually accompanied me on the motorcycle up the road to Roberta's house at the top of the Scopeti woods. My friend and I would do our daily walk, catch up on the Fiorentina soccer club (Roberta was sure, when I was in town, the team would win more) and affairs outside of the "Scopeti". I just needed to get away. While I dreaded the comments Roberta would make on the latest Bush fiasco, I could not seem to move my legs fast enough up the hill to the comfort of Roberta Degli'Innocenti.

There is nothing like the warmth and reassurance of a friend that can give us the strength to ward off the evils of people with little to do with their lives but make-up and manicures. Once I was through with my walk I had a plan. I would rid myself of the nagging nail in my forehead.

ଔ୬

If one were to know the day that their relationship would turn from loving to sour would they avoid that day? Or is it like the habitual dieter that slowly creeps to 50 pounds over what she weighed on her wedding day, never really knowing the day it

happened? Would it be possible to re-set, to re
kindle and fix things before it was too ugly?

I know the answer. No one sees it coming. It seeps
into your life like dampness in the foundation of a
stone Tuscan cottage. If I were to pinpoint where
the fairytale turned tragedy, the instances are many,
some clouded by selective memories, others like
sharp pangs of hunger that you would like to ignore,
fueled by the tongues of those around you. Still,
they are there, you just don't see where they came
in from until it is too late or too sorry. I can forgive
but I have forgotten much or this slow seeking of
rot into the foundation of our marriage.

One year when Kikka was small, we had passed a
tumultuous Autumn. Kikka barely a year old had
Scarlettina a form of Scarlet fever. Later she got
Whooping cough and our closeness would have it
that while I had been vaccinated in the states for this
childhood ailment, at twenty-four, I got it too. Then
there was one of us almost getting killed in our
respective commutes: Orazio 100KM to Siena and
me 120 KM to Empoli each way that it seemed
impossible that we would survive the winter.

We did. Mezzano was paradise on earth Sandro our
dear friend and partner in real estate had said when
he and Orazio had bought it years before. They had
gotten a deal on it as it was built without permits
and was nestled high in the hills above Strada in
Chianti on the way to Poggia La Croce under the
Castle of the Cintoia. While the seclusion was
welcome in their single days for wild parties and
naked relaxation. It was not idyllic for a young
"stranger" wife. Especially not one that spent most
of her designing days alone without telephone and
the nearest town seven KM away.

The Other Side of Tuscany

The pregnancy of Kikka high-risk and in the twilight of two previous miscarriages did finally ignite the phone company into action stringing the land line to our home like a Napolitano clothes-line. It came with the condition we dig the last 100 meter ditch from the gate to our front door to lay the last bit of line in the cleared piazza in front of our home.

I can still see the glistening backs of Sandro and my husband with picks and hoes as they worked hacking in the sun to link me to civilization and a doctor if the case need be. Next they concentrated on water.

They purchased the pond that was spring-fed by the Cintoia and formed a consortium with the 28 people who owned homes on the hill, mainly as second homes. Water, I had reminded my husband was the one element no matter how creative I could not do without.

When the pump broke our last summer at Mezzano, the twins barely six months old and Kikka three, I tested just how much I could do without water. With a blow up canoe and a couple bottles of Vernaccia[4], I bathed the children. I brushed my teeth with the finest Chianti and cleaned my pores with Vin Santo[5]. I drew the line with flushing toilets with wine, some things are just holy.

---

[4] **Vernaccia** is a white Italian wine, made from the Vernaccia grape, produced in and around the Italian town of San Gimignano. It is the oldest and noblest of white wines and the first white to receive DOC status in 1966.

[5] **Vin Santo** meaning *holy wine* is an Italian dessert wine. This traditional Tuscan wine is made from Trebbiano and Malvasia grapes, and is typically very sweet.

We moved that August. The love affair with our Paradise on Earth ended with the need to flush our toilets.

CB80

The wonderful thing about small towns is, with a handful of details, you can get as much information as an expert search engine spider.

I used what little I had, to seek out this incorrigible gossip and his wife, and set the record straight. I came to their home unannounced and to their embarrassment, carrying all their lies in my breast. I did what I had come to do.

It would be two years before Orazio would know where I went that afternoon after my walk with Roberta. It would be two years before together, we would see the matchmaker at the market and he would mention our lovely afternoon together.

Amazing how memory corrects what we remember when our lies are laid out with our tea.

Out beyond ideas of wrongdoing
and right doing is a field. I'll meet
you there.

~Rumi

Chapter 31: Too Close to Home

Cary, North Carolina, USA 2008

I waited with anticipation for my younger sister Sherry and Jalen to arrive at the Sweet Tomatoes for our Saturday evening out for dinner and a movie. When they finally arrived Jalen ran up to me like a snake oil salesman sees a crowd, he proceeded to retail the latest happenings in his life. His school week had been uneventful but his cousin Nickie and he were going to be on the same soccer team.

He was brimming with reviews and information about the upcoming feature we were about to see. I guess it was the happiness I felt being with my nephew and his joie-de-vivre, that my observation was clouded, as we walked in and I hardly noticed the school bus yellow flyer on the door.

"You're missing Aunt Nancy. Look!" as he transitioned from "Nickie plays *Forward* and I play *Defense*" and started pointing to the flyer on the door.

How do adults go missing? Maybe she was sick, maybe she ran away with a lover; maybe she just did not want to be found. I had had those thoughts myself a hundred times before. I had made a mental note to Google *Nancy Cooper* when I returned that evening.

Never had I imagined when I found the "missing Nancy" that I too would find my own personal hell unearthed from a carefully seeded corner of my past. The damp corners, held my own "missing Nancy" and when I read that her friend had called 911 hoping to save her friend, I bowed my head in prayer and thanked God for Mary Flannigan. In the months that followed and the case unraveled, I shuddered as I listened to her friend's 911 calls imagining my own friend's courage that November morning on the phone.

Then I remembered how I sat on the bed that morning. A million thoughts had rushed to me. My cheek was burning and my left eye felt as if it would pop right out of my face, not so much for the blow, but just to get out of the room.

I knew I needed to get out of his way but still I sat. He called Italy. He cursed me to a voice on the other side of the world. Probably his lover or sister or God, I did not care, let him kill me then I could rest.

My thoughts flashed to him banging on the windows of my Four Runner when I still lived in Tuscany. I had locked the kids and me inside to get away from him whenever the temperature changed. Then, the horror of finally backing the car away from the house and rounding the corner of our property to get to the iron gate, only to realize that he had removed the pin and the electric opener would not work.

ಬು The Other Side of Tuscany ೞ

I had been trapped and soon he appeared from the rosemary hedge that surrounded the lower portion of the house, shielding us from the old mill property on the river that belonged to Maria Barboni. I had hoped the hedge would split and give the curious neighbor vista to our domestic hell, so that she could come and help me.

While the children thought it was some sort of game when he stood in front of the car, we all screamed. I laid on the horn to see if Maria would come to the window he always hated scandal and soon his cousins were gathering at the windows above and Maria was walking up to the street.

No one came that day to help us. They never did and sometimes the beast would go away and my husband would return.

It is so hard to know when to act, when the truth is draped in vows and your friends are in danger. Friends, true friends smell danger just as horses smell the rain before it comes. Sadly, the victims themselves can stare danger in the face over coffee and never see what a friend risks friendship to prevent. That is why friends react, are called to action while victims and the families sit paralyzed in fear and indecision. In many ways, that is why friends save us from ourselves and our families think everything will be fine, if we just don't mention it.

ೞಬು

That time I had done nothing wrong. How did I know my former rogue lover would be calling and disrupting the marriage cart that had been so carefully righted, the ripened fruit placed back as

not to rot by our eldest daughter? I hoped my heart
would give out and remove me from this room, this
life, this problem that had no solution. The blood
was trickling from my right nostril. It was my blood
pressure and the room started to dot like a flash
camera.

It all started with a phone call. Rewind. Please God
rewind.

God did not hear my prayers for Nancy Cooper.

Sadly, as the young woman's body was pulled from
a water collection pond a few days later, I grieved
not only the young mother and her loving family
but her friends who had watched her life from
behind the glass and could not stop this tragedy.
Mary had broken the "glass" that morning my
estranged husband had come calling at 101 Main
Street.

Friends do that for friends, they give a rat's ass of
the mess that will be created. Family is afraid of the
shards, unless they can be swept under a rug.

I was an exuberant child who embarked on an
extraordinary adventure diving into the Fashion
Realm, but then never fully realized my dreams
forfeited for love, for him. Now, I had neither one
nor the other and I was not even sure if I wanted to
be on this earth any more.

Nothing made any sense. Like a gambler who felt
all was going his way to only find that he had lost
his life's work, I felt a suicidal plunge… and
welcomed it. My life exemplified the painful
journey from marital certainty to existential doubt
that comes with the defining experience called

infidelity. Not only do you lose the sense of wife but also that sense of self.

There is some madness in love. But there is also always some reason in madness.

~Friedrich Nietzsche

Chapter 32: House of Madness

Gli Scopeti, Tuscany, Italy 2006

I arrived in Pisa from London Gatwick and looked about to find that the line I needed to stand in was considerably shorter than that of the others. I guess there were perks to being a stranger after all. The ECC and English filed around in a long curve and I simply walked up to the counter and presented my passport. The young man looked bored and while his uniform was well pressed and clean he looked like someone had rolled him out of bed and shoved him into the glass box that contain him and all his authority.

"Quanto trattiene?" How long will you stay he asked, why do you care I wondered?

I had clearly passed the scrupulous English immigration. There was a time that this question would follow with the asking of a good number to reach me or if I wanted to wait around until the end of their shift. Sometimes the polizia would congregate like a pack of hungry wolves looking at a tender sheep. I did not mind the rite of passage that age now granted me.

The Other Side of Tuscany

I looked at the glass and saw the reflection of myself. Without make up and no sleep for twenty-four hours, I was still fresher looking than most of the younger women on the flight that had merely flown in from England. I said a prayer of gratitude to my mother and grandmother for their gifts.

The thump of the stamp on my passport startled me and shook me from my thoughts. I realized that the earlier question had been an attempt at conversation and not protocol. "Enjoy - Italy - Pretty - Woman" He smiled. And I smiled too; I guess I was not as old as I felt.

As I left the baggage claim I saw him, Orazio was there hurrying about and whistling like he does when he is nervous. He was careful not to look at me too closely and measured was his emotion yet he was curious to size me up, as the other men were doing. That is his way, but I see it now what I always thought was that he did not care was really that he did not know how to act .Every reunion was the sign that there would be another departure. Every encounter, a painful reminder of the goodbyes and the tears, the ripping of children from arms that ached to hold for one more day, lips that wanted to kiss one more night. The plans that had no clear path or true beginning

It used to be I would come and there had been some attempt at normalcy. Walking in this time I found my two grown children suspended in this menagerie of eccentric behavior.

They too, were running with scissors and at this point, as it were easier to absorb the craziness than fight it. Now all is lost in a battle of what is normal and what is not.

203

I trip over strings and glue and bits of sticks the remnants of a kite making session then in the corner I notice an over-sized skillet - the type that are used to make pasta for 20 - 30 people - dirty with sauce and a few orphaned pieces of pasta. There must have been a party or a wholesale attempt at meal making. There are some of the poetic traces of my last visit, the scented candles and hand woven rugs and placemats. The "order" is there in after thoughts, accented by great big "I live like this now".

The furniture has been moved to accommodate the parties and the Kite work shop however, there are the traces of our memories.

On his last visit to the states he must have found his way to Kinko's armed with his new ears and a words he could actually hear streaming from his mouth he had enlarged the pictures of the children. And now they were stuck on all of the walls of our house, the house of Madness.

In a tender sort of way it touched me but like cheap perfume on an unwelcome guest lingers, so did the European connotation of such a display.

Here, when there was a death of a loved one, these same sorts of manifests papered the streets and avenues with the bereaved. This was to show that once the rain and the elements had washed away the paper the grief would surely leave. His putting them in the house only showed he would grieve the rest of his life the loss of these children.

There were no pictures of me or her for that matter. At one time there was a beautiful picture of the two of them in a frame tucked away in a cabinet where he kept all the pictures of his dear children.

As I thought about it, other than a picture of the two of us that I had painted years ago, I could remember no pictures of us together in 25 years of marriage, and surely none prominently displayed.

This saddened me that for all these years there was nothing to immortalize if not the emotion, at least the beauty of the two of us together because despite the painful undertones, we were a very handsome couple, even today.

At night dreams come and go in the house of madness there is no rest here. At first I thought the home invasions and robberies of years past somehow played on the psyche of those who dwelled there but now the truth is known that that madness that is within him lies in the walls of this house.

My son awakes terrified and screaming he calls for his friends, his pets, his past lover. He tries to save them but cannot. I cry out in arguments and confrontations nightly with co workers, lovers and friends.

It is painful and it is taxing but when the night silences the house the madness stirs and wakes our souls and shakes the dirty secrets we all hold in our chests.

Character like a photograph,
develops in darkness.

~ *Yousuf Karsh*

Chapter 33: Lemons and Elephants

Rossano, Calabria, Italy 2007

I never have been one to see things with a malignant
eye and maybe it is for that reason the hesitation for
the trip to Calabria fell deaf to me. My brother in
law, Fabio, innocent in his own hospitable bid for
the trip was oblivious to the obvious repercussions
that might occur from inviting me to his native
home.

I had never been to Calabria and the entire time I
lived in Italy with my husband, had never been
invited by my in-laws to join them. I was *persona
non grata*, since marrying Orazio and stealing the
fraternal bread-winner from the cure and
maintenance of his sister and her Marquis husband.

I had heard the country was beautiful, savage
compared to the elegance of Tuscany but wild and
jagged, tamed with the warm perfume of lemons
and sweet, sticky bergamot. Calabria was to be
enjoyed in the company of Calabrese. The fate of
the little American, Nicolas Green would chastise
me when I wanted to venture there alone with my
three small children and remind me that Calabria
was a very dangerous place.

❧ The Other Side of Tuscany ☙

Since Anna first became sick with breast cancer fourteen years ago, I was no longer this monster but a survivor. The torch carrier for my father and brother with their cancer crusades, I refused to accept their sentences to die. There were times; their oncologists felt my sheer will was the only thing keeping them alive as there was no real medical explanation.

Anna knew I would not give up on her and stayed with her through those first terrible days after her mastectomy. Her closest friends in their ignorance resigned that she should accept her fate and as if the disease were contagious, deserted her. Instead I snuck into the hospital at night and crawled into her bed not wanting her to be alone with her thoughts, silent enemies in the night. I told her I believed if she had a plan and something to do there was no reason to leave this earth. She worried of her children and I quickly took them in my care. We made plans for her, yes, we made plans for her and in the absence of ideas or depression we made menus for lavish parties.

The trip to Calabria whatever the symbolic underpinnings- had taken on a life of its own. I felt as if I was in a different room from the rest of them and that we were discussing a view but I was at a different window. In my confusion and desire to make this short trip a good one but mostly peaceful and of comfort to Anna, I started to agree that the trip was a poor choice. My reasoning was simple and my motives factual.

Anna would be doing Chemo therapy the day before- how could she possibly feel good enough to drive the 7 and half hours from Florence to Calabria? Fabio had countered that his wife was

ℬ Nancy Stolfo Corti ℛ

strong and that she had felt fine the last time, I think my husband had thought for a moment that I had discovered the ruse, but then almost apologetically he looked at me and then his sister, he knew that I was only doing what I always tried to do and that was, make the best of the situation for everyone else. For that, he was sorry because depending on who we would encounter regardless of the trip, soon I would know the true reason no one wanted the trip to occur while I was there.

The expression, "Everyone tries to act like they don't see the big white elephant in the room" has always brought a smile to my face. You see, my brain draws like an *"etch-a-sketch"* the whimsical expressions and my imagination colors them just as quickly as the lines appear. When my parents first heard the pachyderm expression they were at a Bakers' Convention and their good friend Maxine was telling a story. How shocked they had sounded later that evening as they recounted the story Maxine had told. They were a little confused on how a baker could have an elephant in the room and not cause any problems with the health department.

It would be thirty years later that I would make the connection of how the Cincinnati Baker really did not have an elephant in his basement workshop.

The trip to Calabria discussion seems to have this elephant peeking out from behind the couch every time it was discussed. I really just wanted someone to make the decision for me. I was tired of the mystery solving, too tired to play detective in my own home, too tired to divvy up the teams of friends and foes. I wanted some peace. I had come to give peace. I had come to give a final good bye as an omen that it would not be, just as the many final goodbyes had blessed my brother into countless, priceless, borrowed embraces.

What was silent in the father, speaks in the son, and often I found in the son, the unveiled secret of the father.

~Friedrich Nietzsche

Chapter 34: Of Sons & Dogs

Apex, North Carolina, USA 2008

"Wait, I want you to listen to something…"

Benji interrupted me as I was recounting the last bit of Gemma's game, the house prospects and a great store that had all the wonderful Tuscan foods near Cameron Village. Michele had reminded me on her last trip to Florence that I never finished a sentence or thought completely, without moving onto the next three things popping into my head.

"My God, you are the most ADD person I have ever met you really should be medicated."

Coming from my best friend I guess one should take no offense but then, I had always been this way hadn't she noticed? Maybe the others were the ones that needed to be medicated, yes?

What was that saying about 'Lefties?' *The whole world is born right handed but only the gifted overcome it* maybe that was true with ADD- *The whole world is born focused but only the gifted overcome it?* Sure. I am sure that was it but then why did I always feel a little hurt that I was rambling whenever one of my children told me to focus. I silenced the mental debate for a few beats to catch the first few lines of "Hey Mamma" by Kanye West:

I'm finna take yall back to them better times
I'm finna talk about my mama if yall don't
mind
You work late nights just to keep on the
lights
Mommy got me training wheels so I could
keep on my bike
And you would give anything in this world
And I love you for that mommy cant you
see?

They say there is a connection between mothers and sons. I guess I will never really know if this is true of Benji and me. He is my only son and one that I willed life to just as I had my brother. In many ways, without having ever having spent much time together, they are similar, in ways that only angels can know and mothers understand.

My brother was an avid fisherman not because anyone in our family was but just because one day he decided that he was. Then fashioning a pole from bamboo, he and his friends would fish. He would ride his bike to Hook's pond near the large Tudor Mansions on Philadelphia Drive by the bakery. They would catch frogs and put tadpoles in mason jars, but mostly just sit and wait like fishermen do with lines in the water. He stopped going there when a dead man's decaying body was found in the bushes as he and the Emoff boy dug for worms. He had abandoned fishing a while until he got older and our Lake house proved a much safer venue than the isolated pond.

Benji was more than likely influenced by a Japanese anime' that ran on Italian Television in the afternoon when he was around three or four, Sampei. So it was that in his mind he had the adventures and needs of the Japanese fisherman boy. He never asked for toys and not knowing the true names of equipment would form a vocabulary that I too would imitate when looking for the items in stores.

"Une EN-TRAPOLA Pesci" "A fish Trapper" I would repeat to the shop keeper when he had requested a net one Christmas from Santa Claus. "A RA-PO-LA" giving the name brand of an American Lure an Italian accent because I did not know any better- was another holiday gift giving attempt. I often ended up getting him plush little Teddy bears that would contain a letter to him apologizing for not being what he had asked and telling him a story about why they decided to come and play with him instead.

Only when the much desired Iguana did not arrive one Christmas did he show a hint of disappointment as two chubby tears slip down his chocolate chip cheeks and onto the letter of the dark brown bear. Even when his sisters received many gifts under the tree, Benji never complained. The ones he had were often homemade: wooden swords, bows and arrows with real Robin Hood leather hats and fishing poles with safety pin hooks.

He was a simple child with an old soul and wise reasoning. The white lies of childhood that hide magic and wonder would have to have evidence to get past even the youngest Benji. Every Christmas I would don heavy work boots that Beppe Gambassi had left when they finished the restructuring of Gli

Scopeti, climb into the massive stone fireplace and jump out with soot covered boots while silently saying *"with a bound"* Then I proceeded to track soot foot prints all through the house and out the front door and into the night.

As we knelt on the kitchen floor
I said mommy Imma love you till you don't
hurt no more
And when I'm older, you aint gotta work no
more
And Imma get you that mansion that we
couldn't afford
See you're, unbreakable, unmistakable
Highly capable, lady that's makin loot
A livin legend too, just look at what heaven
do
Send us an angel, and I thank you (Hey
Mama)

The au pairs hated my Christmas ritual that included putting together bicycles and stuffing oversized packages, fully wrapped into the flue of the fireplace in the middle of the night after having worked long hours at the restaurant. Though I had even longer hours than the girls I found the baking and cooking for the large Christmas dinner that our patrons had booked weeks in advance- therapeutic. Wasn't the whole restaurant thing for me anyway? It was a gift from my husband when he found out that I would be giving up my career after the birth of the twins. My husband, in his naiveté had thought that I would be bored after staying home with three small children and would need something to do- a restaurant at the time seemed a perfect solution.

"You do dinner parties all the time, what's the difference? Now, they pay to have dinner at your house."

I have to admit the theory was good but after a few horrific nights of unplanned swarms of diners or an unannounced health inspector the seemingly simple solution to our problems was not that simple.

Our children cried when I descended the stairs at night. Many nights they came into the kitchen to be confronted by an angry man that had taken over their father's body. Some nights they would sneak into the restaurant like lost kittens and hide on benches and fall asleep. The waiters and I would carry them up the stone steps and into their beds. In the silent, angry ritual of remaking the dining room presentable again and eating our two am dinner, we would say little. Much was said during the service, much was irrevocable and like the wooden fence post to which nails are driven by mistake and removed, the kind words and fine bottles of wine did not fill the holes that were left by the abuse only hours before.

Benji would wake as I creaked up the stairs hearing my lame toes and ankles cracking on the stone steps. He always had a question or something that he pondered, "Ma Perche?" Had I know the beauty of the internet and its wealth of knowledge I surely could have silenced him with its promise, but in the absence of this invention a trip to the Biblioteca (Library) would be confirmed if my answer was not adequate or without evidence.

I wondered now how he could have missed *the evidence*. He had gone back every summer. He had been there through the longest and most serious of the affairs. My children had learned to tread lightly in the craziness that had become our lives. Benji and Kikka fluttered back and forth over whether or not I should move on.

"Mom your still good looking" Benji had said "and not *that* old." one year driving home to Ohio.

The *"that"* was a little too strong to be convincing. Only Gemma was unfaltering in her convictions that Babbo[1] was forever and we were only made one for the other. Though part of me wanted the limbo to end every time I thought "this is it" the incredible sadness washed over me like cancer and I knew she was right.

Anything worth having was never easy.

With all the pain of our relationship, I was always the one who was scrutinized- my sins- large and on display, much like my personality took center stage. Dr Johnson had once shared a book she was writing, something about "this is my brain on Hollywood." In it was a passage on how people tend to sabotage themselves when they are successful because they are afraid or when things are going too good, they feel that it will soon disappear so they ruin it first.

In reality, while my brain did not have much Hollywood, my life sure did. I was probably more misunderstood than outrageous and the details amplified to satisfy a good tale. I had become larger than life in my absence and those that were unsure of me before now disliked me with fervor. My children had become more and more critical of me with every trip home to Tuscany. My quirks were

---

[1] Tuscan for *daddy.*

now sins, my non-conformities reduced to being ignorant. More specifically, an ignorant American- and with that- I single handedly became responsible for a population of plaid pants wearers, that drank cappuccino after dinner and spoke louder hoping the English would somehow translate at higher octaves into Italian.

"Benji, like the dog?" was the reaction from the nurse when I finally was able to name my son.

No, like my son, the little Rambo in the incubator that has fought the last 24 hours for his life and is still looking for his twin, can't you see?

I had wanted to choke the woman. I already had heard her commenting to one of the others how much he looked like E.T. and how I was out of my head for checking out of the hospital with a fever. If she only knew this was my only alternative to seeing and protecting the son that was almost lost in birth.

"Figli Maschi" the son everyone toasts and waits for, the son full of promises more than the daughters, the son that was taken away without a name and without hope. If only she knew what mothers know in the protecting and saving of all our children, not just our sons.

Now, I forgive her. As I sit here and look at the young man driving his "mamma" to Red Lobster for our date, a tear streaming down his face, as listening to the song he relives our survival together, I realize that she was right. I mentally remove the pins from the nurse voodoo doll placed years before.

Benji opens his heart and his life without judgment. So what if he had the evidence? He saw something greater in the "storia" that had played out for him between fireworks and beach trips, wood oven pizzas and late night runs to Petriolo[2]. He saw happiness where there had been sadness, laughter where there had been loneliness. I know in his heart he felt nothing less of his father or of me.

Benji loves unconditionally.

He was just being Benji, like the dog.

---

[2] Geyser fed spa naturally cut in a river bed in the heart of wild Tuscany (Marema).

The deeper that sorrow carves into
your being, the more joy you can
contain.

~Kahlil Gibran

Chapter 35: Sorrow

Apex, North Carolina, USA 2009

Some days I wonder if the unhappiness I have
endured in my marriage is the reason that I enjoy
life so fully. I wonder if it is the reason that the
moments of happiness are measured so tall and so
richly wide. It is hard for those who read into my
life to understand the stick I use to measure with, is
my own. While my yardstick cannot possibly
measure a credit score or rate a Hollywood wife,
mine is a true measure for my life; one that shakes
the breath out of every day and touches the life of
someone with gratitude and forgiveness, creativity
and laughter.

To the embarrassment of my children, I cannot pass
a hula- hoop in any store without trying it out and I
will walk whole stretches of shoreline with
seashells for my eyes. And elevators, the silent
tombs for conversation? They become game shows
for me where willing contestants ride and those not
so willing can't wait for the doors to open to their
floor. It is a shame that more and more, I have to
curb my childlike enthusiasm as people are
increasingly afraid of people who care to make
perfect strangers smile. It saddened me that so many

❧ The Other Side of Tuscany ❧

of the years with Orazio were silent ones, afraid of how sharp our words would be.

"Mom I do not want to put a bug in your ear," my eldest daughter ventured, "but I am wondering… I think Dad may be seeing someone again. I mean I don't want you to worry and Walter and I will certainly bring you back information after the trip but I just want…"

Wanted what? I have stopped keeping score. Loving Orazio as much as I do, I find comfort in knowing someone is taking care of him. I don't want to know who this person is or if they stand for anything. I feel sorry for her because she will never be me. I am special beyond black and white, as are my children. If we are alone on the other side, so be it, we have tried.

Kikka stumbled through relationships always afraid of what would lurk if she loved completely and trusted totally, just as I did. My son teetered on rules for men and rules for love. My youngest, Gemma only skirted the fringes, never trusting, never loving and never risking, at least not ever telling, if she did.

If there was another woman I would tell her: Do not wake me in the morning. Do not patronize me with your compliments or discredit me with your insults. I do not want to hear about your sexual escapades and when you can no longer have him because he has tired of you and has moved on to someone younger, please do not call me to cry on my shoulder. I have no more tears for this.

Wives should not have to be there, for the mistresses no matter the circumstances. The only

219

tears that wait for me are those of my nephews' hat tricks, home runs and graduations. I save my tears for my children and their successes, the weddings and grandchildren who will come. There are no tears for you faithful companion and discarded lover.

I learned late that forgiveness is a healthy alternative and could give strength for another day; the scoreboard is harder to maintain. I measure in that for which I am grateful: defining moments and closeness to the essence of a life a mistress will never visit not even in her dreams - not jewelry and photographs or what her shallow girlfriends say will give her passage. Her words will never penetrate the love that protects a family bond, in the passion for a greater good, a larger whole. Even drowning with photographs and notebooks documenting the love we shared and knowing this, I can still love life and it loves me.

Maybe in some odd way, I am like the dying girl: everything is brighter and sharper and filled with beauty. I see opportunity for opening that line from one heart to the next, in everyone. I live to tie a bow from the satin cord that connects all humanity. It is for this reason that my choices have been made through rhinestone studded glasses with a plastic nose and not sophisticated spectacles.

Revenge, morphine for the hopeless, is not my motive, hope and humor are. Armed with my outlook on life as a dog, I push forward. Unconditionally.

Memory is a child walking along
the seashore. You never can tell
what small pebble it will pick up
and store away among its treasured
things.

~Pierce Harris

Chapter 36: Treasured Things

Florence, Tuscany, Italy 2007

One-side of the story is a bad thing. Or is it?

It was this morning at the market that I started to feel insignificant again, caught in our love rekindling yet ill-equipped for the journey. My husband loved the open market and wanted to make sure I got in some great bargain hunting before I left. The cheese vendor had begun:

> *Who knows not that wine is, as Cinciglione and Scolaio and many another aver, an excellent thing for the living creature, and yet noxious to the fevered patient? Are we, for the mischief it does to the fever-stricken, to say that 'tis a bad thing? Who knows not that fire is most serviceable, nay, necessary, to mortals? Are we to say that, because it burns houses and villages and cities, it is a bad thing?*

The quote was from Giovanni Boccaccio a 14th century writer whose themes centered on love, fortune and ingenuity. Ironically, I had spent the last few months toying with ditching the whole book thing back into the drawer. It was "a bad thing" to talk of such things my daughter Kikka and sisters had said. Now a perfect stranger was quoting a passage as if to reach out and quiet my concerns, in doing so awakened other demons: my inadequacies. I hurry upstairs as an eruption of emotion has paralyzed me with the simple task of organizing a drawer before I leave again.

Lately, when winds of contrasting emotions lash at me my relief is binge writing. This necessary catharsis of pain, much like the bloodletting of a swollen limb, allows me to continue. The relief is almost instant - "the healing" nothing but imaginary yet it allows for another day, another year or what seems like another life, to continue.

The galloping horse of memories tramples me in its passing, I take inventory of what to report and what to ignore. I have to acknowledge the passing. I can no longer ignore what has made me the person I am today and continue to hide who I am from my children. Where they see ruin and a pile of ash, I see the brilliance of a life well-lit and a life that will rise again. Then need to remember the beauty of their childhood and not let the shadow of the last few years, dim the memories. They need to have that hope that comes with survival and growth, just as I do.

Twelve years ago almost to the date I left behind my dreams and vows, in hopes of cultivating them in America, just as my parents had done. It seemed impossible to grow anything in Tuscany. Our union and our united, aligned destinies had been seeded in a soil poisoned by a catastrophic karma or was it love?

Spellbound, dangerous love, coupled with a healthy dose of superstition. Much like the dog, beaten within an inch of his life, nestles back to the very the person responsible for his wounds, we fed on the disastrous omen "that we would be miserable for the rest of our lives" should we end up together. In our togetherness, most of our marriage was apart. The miserable of our marriage was anointed by a woman's scorn, and brought the worst of my husband and me. As if we had no right to be happy and when there was happiness, it was over shadowed by a feeling it would never last.

I still dream of the days of happiness of that first year in the rustic 1400th century chapel converted to our home, *La Casina.* I know we can break the curse, if we let go and forgive.

There was no rhyme or reason to the enchantment Tuscany holds over those who venture to break off a piece and sample. There was no rhyme or reason before the internet and technology, nonetheless these advancements had made for a sweeter transition.

Research was done over a glass of wine or at the dinners of intellects and blue bloods. Such was the culture of the common masses that to find a farmer in his field quoting Dante or to have a home schooled seamstress recognize the masters of Italian painting was common place. These revelations let my self-consciousness and inadequacies overwhelm me even on my better of days. The image of me pulling my pants down and peeing on a sheriffs' shoes, a constant reminder of how close we all are to not being able to deal with our demons any more.

I was the center of attention in our smallish town. With the absence of YouTube and Scarlet to poke fun at, "strangers" were a reasonable alternative for the void in their lives between after dinner and the espresso al bar. When the limelight was too much; my husband took it upon himself to make sure he humbled me. Soon, most of those present would add to the criticism and jeering and making fun of either how I was dressed or how my hair was that particular evening. I would be haunted later thinking of Caterina, I had my children who thought of me as a wizard and the magic would melt the meanness, but she had no magic, no children. The alchemy of Bacchus was the only magic she had.

I thought for years that he was cruel and manipulative since the arguments that ensued were finished with glorious hours filled with sex and fine wine. A twisted ritual and soon all was forgotten. Couldn't we by-pass the argument and just have the sex and wine? Would it have not been just as enjoyable? Maybe not, sorrow makes for spaces that greater joys fill. I was tired of being so joyful.

Later, I realized that the women at these dinners were far more cultured than the average catty cow even at the highest level of my industry, just not as worldly. My barefaced experience as a globetrotter and young designer coupled with a language not quite mastered, made me look like a braggart or a liar. Now I see these women were not mean spirited, they just did not know any better. My husband's interruptions served to warp the situation some but the level of interest was so irresistible that whenever someone had the opportunity to talk to me, they did. It really was not a conversation but an interrogation. Just the same, the inquiry was a quiz, a game show of humiliation, a precursor to reality

TV. Whenever I felt they would not let me off the hook for my lack of knowledge on Boccaccio or Ghibillini and Guelfe - I reverted to the coy and stupid American who delighted them and irritated my husband even more.

He hated that I was "smart", his friends reminded him, "you wanted an intelligent wife - oh pedal her," referencing the Italian expression - *"you want a bicycle, now pedal it."* I asked questions as often as a small child and though it sometimes irritated him, he loved to tell me and teach me about the richness of the country we both enjoyed. He loved our conversations almost, as much as our sex. Sadly "our language" was one that was interpreted poorly over water and through airwaves. Sadly, distance and time our enemies, in a language perfected by all our senses not just our ears. The hand and lip reading, the dusty volume on the shelf pulled down and opened for reference, the bottle of wine that had lost its color and looked like cloth in the bottom, were lost despite the many technological advances and despite the enthusiasm of the initial quest. It is no surprise that his infidelity was aroused not only by a lack of sex, as much as, the need for a meaningful conversation.

I could make it right: I had girlfriends, I had children and I had e-mail. I was sure I had figured out the other side of the conversation.

Unchain my heart, release the letter
in my soul and let me start living
again.

~Nac

Chapter 37: Stay

Raleigh, North Carolina, USA 2009

Linda stumbled though speaking her mind, "I was cleaning my house and I had on my play list this song….It is by Sugarland …something like 'will you stay or'..." A few very loud two fingered key strokes ensued. I quickly found the song she had mentioned.

"It is called 'Stay'," I say.

Not expecting me to have the words in front of me before she could defend why she was calling almost apologetically she interjects , "Well I heard this song…and I…" she began to cry and before I knew it tears were rolling down my face too.

I had barely looked at the words.

Lately, be it the onset menopause or a nervous breakdown we, the three sisters (le sorelle materasse[1] Orazio liked to call us) were a slobbering puddle of emotions even if it was just a television commercial. I had always been the "emotional one." My sisters had always managed to

---

[1] The slang term for the sculpture, "Le Grazie", the Three Graces.

❧ The Other Side of Tuscany ❧

hold it together. Now we were all becoming emotional. Even our father with the treatments for his prostate cancer was becoming "Zia Theresa[2]. Emotional", testy, nosey Zia Theresa was "just menopause" before we knew what hormones did.

We were all in some form or another suffering from hormones, stress, the economy and the last thing anyone wanted was another emotional blow-out caused by yours truly. "No more tears" was not just baby shampoo, it was a family mantra.

There was beauty in tears and I shed them freely in happiness and not so happy times. In sharing and in withholding. Lives without tears are lives clothed so tightly they no longer feel what is around them. Maybe menopause is God's way of letting us shed some of our clothes so we can feel again?

"This song made me think of you and Orazio - and I know you are writing this book and I know it is important for you. But I think you need to put your energy into your future and not into the past. Just let it go."

I felt like someone was slamming my fingers into the drawer again; the drawer I had so carefully and meticulously opened, sorted and cleaned so that I could share its contents. A drawer that contained weapons of a war I never started and gowns for a party not yet attended; the hat and gloves for tea on an English lawn of a past held in my heart. The drawer was in order now. I could share it. The

---

2. Zia Theresa was my father's beautiful, spinster aunt who finally married in her late 50s because no one was good enough for her. She was very critical and expected perfection in all and all things.

choice was left to the reader if they wanted to know what it contained.

Silence.

"I mean you are putting so much energy into this…"

I was only half listening partly because I was thinking about everything that had been going right for about a month and then all of the sudden everything was going terribly wrong.

Did I even have the mental bandwidth? It certainly was nice that she was giving me a pass. Linda was good that way. She had become the glue of our family, a position I once held. I was sorry for this. I never wanted her to taste anything that was bitter. I never wanted her to have to see with my eyes. As an optometrist she knew our prescriptions were the same, as a sister she knew I looked at everything through a kaleidoscope. She would not participate in my ever-changing view of color and design.

I was sorry she was feeling this sadness for me and much as I wanted to protect her, I felt it was not fair to keep doing so.

Everything was going to get really bad before it got better. I did not even have the money to publish a Lulu copy. Only my closest friends knew this. I had felt that at one point, I had willed the US economy into this crazy tail spin, by my own testing of how flawed a system it was.

Anora McGaha had worked for months without a dime, accepting checks she couldn't cash and putting them into a sacred coffer. She helped absolve my guilt for not paying her up front. The gesture let her know that I valued her work, but mostly it was that I valued this spiritual being God had sent to me, much as Renata was sent to save Kikka from the logics and bring her into this life. How mocking life can be, my non-conformity is the very reason Kikka exists, yet she cannot understand how I cannot do what I am told? Anora had been sent to birth this book, to stoke the cinders and start my life again.

There would be many more play lists and many more tears. But if we cannot look the past in the face we cannot move on to the future. My father had always told me to face my fears; much as I tried, they often returned in my dreams for review.

Still we must keep going. If we never go to investigate the shadow protruding from behind the door we will not know that it is just be a mop and not a serial killer. Is it worth never entering that room and not knowing?

"I really think you just need to forget it. I mean write it but don't put so much energy into it; do it for yourself, you know…"

I looked at the words and tried to have a listen but only found other songs. I read on another site and listened a bit but it was a little too country to be my song - our song. I didn't quite understand how my sister could make the connection between my husband and me? Then, I could see my husband jittering like he was doing a "do-see-do" around the kitchen with me and I started to laugh. I remembered how I always wanted to dance with him and in moments of our aloneness we did. Those moments were the wind that stoked my ashes.

I remembered back to when *Malia* was opened
during that first August and not a single guest
booked a table. Orazio and I had turned the lights
down and lit a fire in the stone fireplace in the
middle of the rustic vault of the main dining room.
He held me close and safe as we danced to Etta
James and Frank Sinatra. Through the opened arch
at the end of the restaurant I could see the purple
glow of evening above the blackened silhouette of
the Scopeti Forest. It had been magical in its
simplicity. As I looked in the eyes of my husband
the sparkle told me I was his and the tears told me
he wished there was more that he could do.

How I want now to tell him that is all I wanted. One
half turn revealed that we had an audience, a walker
from Monte Buoni gathering some coolness before
dinner had stopped to watch us dance in the glow of
our August fire. Since the road was higher than the
wine-cellared cove, the man had to stoop as if he
were about to enter our tender, glowing grotto.

"Ma che fa freddooooh?" extending the final "oh"
in Toscannaccio he was asking us if we were cold.
The beauty I thought he observed was not us and
the spell we shared, but that we had lit a fire in
August. In speaking out he broke the flask that
contained our precious moment.

Wasteful like precious Chianti running over
terracotta tiles, my husband answered with a
surrendering, apologetic shrug to this stranger,
"Awww you know how these Americans are…"

And with that he had turned up the lights and closed
the door.

The Other Side of Tuscany

My husband's "not standing up" for our moments were betrayals just as deep as those of infidelity, though I would venture that these reasons would seldom enter the courtroom as a motive for divorce.

Moments like these give me insight into the expression,
"Maledette Toscani." *Damn Tuscans. Damn that man.* Damn Orazio too, for not sticking up for his heart.

I was laughing and then I was crying as I read the words. Finally I found the Sugarland video on YouTube with beautiful ballads and lead singer Jennifer's earthy, wonderful voice.

She looked into my eyes as she sang into the camera. I started to cry and in that moment a tear rolled down her face too. The voice-over kept singing and the camera panned to her and then the guitarist. They chose to capture and not edit out "our" personal pain. I had done the same with this book. She had felt my pain, I felt the sting of that first, "he just left here," hit me hard in the face. I couldn't watch her; even the guitarist seemed to want to look away. Was he the reason? I thought he looked up as if to say he was sorry. I recovered to hear her tell the man she addressed in the song:

So next time you find
you wanna leave her bed for mine
Why don't you stay?
I'm up off my knees
I'm so tired of being lonely
You can't give me what I need
When she begs you not to go
There is one thing you should know

231

I don't have to live this way
Baby, why don't you stay?

I pulled out my laptop and accessed the file *Book Research*. The first file was dated February 1, 2005, its working title, *Infidelity*; it opened with this quote from Peter Ustinov.

"Love is an act of endless forgiveness, a tender look which becomes a habit."

That's where it started, *Infidelity,* but that is not what it means to me now. Eleajora, Bud and maybe hundreds in between did us both a favor by giving us back ourselves.

It is sad to forget a lover but it is a tragedy to forget ourselves.

It wasn't about revenge. It was about healing. It was about forgiving and second chances. It was about having our memories back, and not nightmares and voids of time that were so painful we cannot remember even what was good about our lives.

This was a beautiful, defining moment that I *can* savor now. I sip it slowly like a wine from the cellar that has been prepared, decanted and aired. I understand the roughness, as well as, the roundness. This is and was my life, our lives together and apart - after all.

I accessed the file we had worked on yesterday and started typing. My forehead aches and I rub the place where I landed on a hard plastic Nancy Nurse [3] one night, forever reminding me of that bad dream

---

[3] A popular talking doll in the early 60s was received on Christmas in 1963 from my uncle Dan.

and falling on to the floor; the pain never really goes away.

What was my sister telling me? To just give up and move on? I can't. I know this woman; the singer of this sad ballad has felt the pain, our pain. Maybe you have too. She lets the blood from her wound and so do I.

Anger is toxic; forgiveness heals and blinds you to the weapons lovers bring.

The slap of infidelity hits you harder than any man ever can. It knocks you to your knees and you grapple for a friend and for safety. The rules state that it's over, but your heart tells you that it's not. There are oceans for your tears and in the end no one will know the difference whether you go or stay.

Tears are only salty water. Salty water kills plants but it disinfects wounds and cooks pasta.

The choice is yours.

The choice is yours.
When spider webs unite, they can
tie up a lion.

~Ethiopian Proverb

Reflections

When you decide to spend your life with someone, you share your life with them. All of it - despite the parts that you did not plan or expect - you share it and spend it together.

What is important are the lessons we learn from the struggles we endure.

This is not a tale of infidelity or divorce Italian style. This is a lesson from life that can be applied to business, children and our selves.

Just because something is not perfect - does it mean it is not good?

No, imperfection has a place in all of us.

My life, my story is about second chances… and third and fourth chances. It is not about giving up despite how weak you feel. Even the weakest threads of spiders can tie up a lion if they unite. Gather your silken threads and remember who you are; there is strength in the mirror before you.

There is power in forgiveness just as there is rebirth after every storm. However, you do have to shoulder the burden of removing the wreckage to allow the light to pass through, even if it is only the cracks.

The Other Side of Tuscany

You will need friends and you will need strangers whose unexpected kind words or flowers will make your heart sing for another hour, another day.

You will need sadness to appreciate the happiness you had so carelessly set aside like a dress out of fashion. Try it back on and be amazed at how beautiful it is. You will get through the darkest of days and the lowest of lows, just remember who you are and be grateful.

Remember not everyone measures with the same stick; not every clock holds the same time. Your time has come. Be bold, be beautiful. Gather your strengths and if you have none left, gather your friends.

Nancy Stolfo-Corti
Apex, North Carolina, USA
First Edition
December 20, 2009

236

Original Words to Songs

L'Emozione Non a Voce

Io non so parlar d'amore, l'emozione non ha voce
E mi manca un po' il respiro, se ci sei c'è troppa
luce
La mia anima si spande, come musica d'estate
poi la voglia sai mi prende, e mi accende con i baci
tuoi
Io con te sarò sincero,resterò quel che sono
disonesto mai lo giuro,ma se tradisci non perdono
Ti sarò per sempre amico pur geloso come sai
io lo so mi contraddico ma preziosa sei tu per me

Tra le mie braccia dormirai
serena..mente ed è importante questo sai
per sentirci pienamente noi

Un'altra vita mi darai, che io non conosco
la mia compagna tu sarai,fino a quando so che lo
vorrai
Due caratteri diversi,prendon fuoco facilmente
ma divisi siamo persi,ci sentiamo quasi niente
Siamo due legati dentro,da un amore che ci dà
la profonda convinzione,che nessuno ci dividerà

Un'altra vita mi darai,che io non conosco
la mia compagna tu sarai fino a quando lo vorrai
poi vivremo come sai,solo di sincerità
di amore e di fiducia,poi sarà quel che sarà
Tra le mie braccia dormirai serenamente
ed è importante questo sai
per sentirci pienamente noi
pienamente noi

Testo La Lontananza

Mi ricordo che il nostro discorso
fu interrotto da una sirena
che correva lontana, chissà dove?
Io ebbi paura perche sempre
quando sento questo suono,
penso a qualcosa di grave
e non mi rendevo conto, che per me e per te,
non poteva accadere in nulla di più grave,
del nostro lasciarci . . .
allora come ora

Ci guardavamo;
avremmo voluto rimanere abbracciati, invece
con un sorriso ti ho accompagnata per la solita
strada.
Ti ho baciata come sempre, e ti ho detto dolcemente
. . .
"la lontananza sai, è come il vento
spegne i fuochi piccoli, ma
accende quelli grandi . . . quelli grandi."

La lontananza sai è come il vento,
che fa dimenticare chi non s'ama
è già passato un anno ed è un incendio
che, mi brucia l'anima.
Io che credevo d' essere il più forte.
Mi sono illuso di dimenticare,
e invece sono qui a ricordare . . .
a ricordare te

La lontananza sai è come il vento
che fa dimenticare chi non s'ama
è già passato un anno ed è un incendio,
che brucia l'anima.

Adesso che è passato tanto tempo,
darei la vita per averti accanto
per rivederti almeno un solo istante
per dirti "perdonami."
Non ho capito niente del tuo bene
ed ho gettato via inutilmente
l'unica cosa vera della mia vita,
l'amore tuo per me

Ciao amore
ciao non piangere
vedrai che tornerò
te lo prometto ritornerò
te lo giuro amore ritornerò
perché ti amo
ti amo
ritornerò
ciao amore
ciao
ti amo

Adesso Tu Lyrics

Nato ai bordi di periferia
Dove i tram non vanno avanti più
Dove l'aria è popolare
È più facile sognare
Che guardare in faccia la realtà...

Quanta gente giovane va via
Acercare più di quel che ha
Forse perché i pugni presi
A nessuno li ha mai resi
E dentro fanno male ancor di più

Ed ho imparato che nella vita
Nessuno mai ci da di più
Ma qaunto fiato quanta salita
Andare avanti senza voltarsi mai...

E ci sei adesso tu
A dare un senso ai giorni miei
Va tutto bene dal momento che ci sei
Adesso tu
Ma non dimentico
Tutti gli amici miei
Che sono ancora là...

E ci si trova sempre più soli
A questa età non sai...non sai
Ma quante corse ma quanti voli
Andare avanti senz'arrivare mai...

E ci sei adesso tu
Al centro dei pensieri miei
La parte interna dei respiri tu sarai
La volontà Che non si limita
Tu che per me sei già
Una rinvicita...

The Other Side of Tuscany

Adesso sai chi è
Quell'uomo che c'è in me...

Nato ai bordi di periferia
Dove non ci torna quasi più
Resta il vento che ho lasciato
Come un treno già passato
Oggi che mi sei accanto
Oggi che si sei soltanto
Oggi che ci sei...
Adesso tu

I can't stand the rain

I can't stand the rain
Against my window
Bringing back sweet memories
I can't stand the rain
Against my window
Because he's not here with me

Hey window pain
Do you remember
How sweet it used to be
When we were together
Everything was so grand
Now that were parted
There's a one sound
That I just can't stand

Chorus
I can't stand the rain
Against my window
Bringing back sweet memories
I can't stand the rain

Le Notte non Finisciano

Inutile parlarne sai
non capiresti mai
seguirti fino all'alba e poi
vedere dove vai
mi sento un po' bambino ma
lo so con te non finirà
il sogno di sentirsi dentro un film.
E poi all'improvviso
sei arrivata tu
non so chi l'ha deciso
m'hai preso sempre più
una quotidiana guerra
con la razionalità
ma va bene purchè serva
per farmi uscire.

Come mai, ma chi sarai
per fare questo a me
notti intere ad aspettarti
ad aspettare te
dimmi come mai, ma chi sarai
per farmi stare qui
qui seduto in una stanza
pregando per un sì.

Gli amici se sapessero
che sono proprio io
pensare che credevano
che fossi quasi un dio
perchè non mi fermavo mai
nessuna storia inutile
uccidersi d'amore
ma per chi?

Chorus

Lo sai all'improvviso
sei arrivata tu
non so chi l'ha deciso
m'hai preso sempre più
una quotidiana guerra
con la razionalità
ma va bene purchè serva
per farmi uscire.

Come mai, ma chi sarai
per fare questo a me
notti intere ad aspettarti
ad aspettare te
dimmi come mai, ma chi sarai
per farmi stare qui
qui seduto in una stanza
pregando per un sì.

The Other Side of Tuscany

Quotes

The brightest future almost always has a forgotten past, once you let go, you will rise like the delicate bubbles of the stomped grapes in your glass. 1

~Nac 1

We can never live in the past as if it were our true home...It is a good thing that God draws this veil over the past even without our asking. In so doing, he allows us to live today and for tomorrow with just the few memories we need of what was. 5

~Karl Barth 5

God put a few wrong people for us to meet. Before we meet the right one, so that when we finally do meet that person, we should be grateful for that gift. 10

~Unknown 10

Never say "Goodbye" when you still want to try, never lose hope unless you are sure of the results. 17

~Nac 17

She not only survived; she became. 22

~Teri Saint Cloud, Bone Sign Arts 22

Driven by the forces of love, the fragments of the world seek each other so that the world may come into being. Love alone is capable of uniting living beings in such a way as to complete and fulfill them, for it alone takes them and joins them by what is deepest in themselves. 26

~Pierre Teilhard de Chardin 26

You may never know the results of your actions but if you do nothing there will be no results. 32

~Mahatma Gandhi 32

Everything that irritates us about others can lead us to an understanding of ourselves. 38

~Carl Jung 38

245

The color of my soul is iron-grey and sad bats wheel about the steeple of my dreams.   42

~Achille-Claude Debussy 42

Life is not the way it's supposed to be. It's the way it is. The way you cope with it is what makes the difference.   45

~Virginia Satir...45

Through the hardest journey we need take but one step at a time but we must keep stepping despite the difficulties.   50

~Chinese Proverb...50

There are two ways of spreading light-to be the candle or the mirror that reflects it.   58

~Edith Wharton 58

Let us be grateful to the people who make us happy; they are the charming gardeners who make our souls blossom.   62

~Marcel Proust...62

If you are going through hell, just keep on going.   68

~Winston Churchill 68

To each other, we were as normal and nice as the smell of bread. We were just a family.   72

~John Irving..72

Discontent is the first step in progress. No one knows what is in him till he tries, and many would never try if they were not forced to.   79

~Basil Maturin..79

A man can be happy with any woman as long as he does not love her.   84

~Oscar Wilde...84

To have great pain is to accept that we also have great heart, amor prossimo and generally give a damn- I think I would not want to be any other way despite the consequences.   91

~Nac..91

The Other Side of Tuscany

Some people move our souls to dance. They awaken us to a new understanding, leave footprints on our hearts and we are never the same. 100

~ Nac 100

Richness is the ability to give not of our possessions but of ourselves and while my accountant would argue, I knew I was the richest people on the planet. 107

~Nac 107

Enjoy this moment in all its fullness, and remember, you are creating your life right now. 113

~Ralph Marston 113

To err is human to forgive is divine. 118

~Alexander Pope 118

Love is an act of endless forgiveness, a tender look which becomes a habit 129

.~Peter Ustinov 129

Never waste jealousy on a real man: it is the imaginary man that supplants us all in the long run. 133

~George Bernard Shaw 133

While the laughter of joy is in full harmony with our deeper life, the laughter of amusement should be kept apart from it. The danger is too great of thus learning to look at solemn things in a spirit of mockery, and to seek in them opportunities for exercising wit. 146

~Lewis Carroll 146

Dreaming permits each and every one of us to be quietly and safely insane every night of our lives. 157

~William Dement 157

Forgiveness is the economy of the heart...forgiveness saves the expense of anger, the cost of hatred, the waste of spirits. 167

~Author Unknown 167

Nancy Stolfo Corti

*I fear one day I'll meet God, he'll sneeze and I won't know
what to say.*   176

~Ronnie Shakes 176

*Jealousy is no more than feeling alone against smiling
enemies.*   185

~Elizabeth Bowen 185

*It's important the people should know what you stand for. It's
equally important that they know what you won't stand for.*
       189

~Mary H. Waldrip 189

*Out beyond ideas of wrongdoing and right doing is a field. I'll
meet you there.*   197

~Rumi 197

*There is some madness in love. But there is also always some
reason in madness.*   202

~Friedrich Nietzsche 202

Character like a photograph, develops in darkness.   206

~ Yousuf Karsh 206

~Friedrich Nietzsche 210

*The deeper that sorrow carves into your being, the more joy
you can contain.*   218

~Kahlil Gibran 218

*Memory is a child walking along the seashore. You never can
tell what small pebble it will pick up and store away among its
treasured things.*   221

~Pierce Harris 221

*Unchain my heart, release the letter in my soul and let me
start living again.*   226

~Nac 226

The Other Side of Tuscany

Locations

Gli Scopeti, Tuscany, Italy *1*

Dayton, Ohio, USA 1963 .... *5*

Dayton, Ohio, USA 1978 .... *10*

Dayton, Ohio, USA 1977 .... *17*

Impruneta, Tuscany, Italy 1980 .... *22*

Impruneta, Tuscany, Italy 1981 .... *26*

Florence, Tuscany, Italy 1982 .... *32*

Milan, Lombardia, Italy 1980 .... *38*

Impruneta, Tuscany, Italy 1981 .... *42*

Impruneta, Tuscany, Italy 1982 .... *45*

Mezzano, Tuscany, Italy 1984 .... *50*

Gli Scopeti, Tuscany, Italy 1992 .... *58*

Gli Scopeti, Tuscany, Italy 1993 .... *62*

Gli Scopeti, Tuscany, Italy1993 .... *68*

Gli Scopeti, Tuscany, Italy 1995 .... *72*

Gli Scopeti, Tuscany, Italy 1995 .... *79*

Apex, North Carolina, USA 1998 .... *84*

Apex, North Carolina, USA 1998 .... *91*

Gli Scopeti, Tuscany, Italy1998 .... *92*

Raleigh, North Carolina, USA 1999 .... *100*

Apex, North Carolina, USA 2004 .... *107*

Apex, North Carolina, USA 2001 .... *113*

249

Apex, North Carolina, USA 2004..................................*118*

Apex, North Carolina, USA 2004..................................*129*

Apex, North Carolina, USA 2004..................................*133*

Gli Scopeti, Tuscany, Italy 2005.................................*146*

Apex, North Carolina, USA 2005..................................*157*

Dayton, Ohio, USA 2007 ....*167*

Apex, North Carolina, USA 2004..................................*176*

Gli Scopeti, Tuscany, Italy 2005.................................*185*

Gli Scopeti, Tuscany, Italy 2005.................................*189*

Cary, North Carolina, USA 2008 ....*197*

Gli Scopeti, Tuscany, Italy 2006.................................*202*

Rossano, Calabria, Italy 2007....................................*206*

Apex, North Carolina, USA 2008..................................*210*

Apex, North Carolina, USA 2009..................................*218*

Florence, Tuscany, Italy 2007....................................*221*

Raleigh, North Carolina, USA 2009...............................*226*

Who's Who

Nancy, Orazio's wife, Kikka, Gemma and Benji's mother

Orazio, Nancy's husband, father to Kikka, Gemma and Benji

Kikka, Nancy's first daughter

Gemma, Nancy's second daughter, twin to Benji

Benji, Nancy's first son, twin to Gemma

Gian, Nancy's older brother

Linda and **Sherry**, Nancy's sisters

Jalen and **Nickie**, Nancy's nephews

Rinaldo, father to Gian, Nancy, Linda and Sherry, Anna's husband, the baker

Anna, (Annabelle) Nancy's mother, the seamstress, Rinaldo's wife, and mother of Gian, Nancy, Linda and Sherry

Rina, Orazio's mother

Anna and Fabio, Orazio's sister and her husband

Sandro, Orazio's best friend

Michele, a classmate of Nancy's from Fashion School in London, a fashion designer still, and dear friend

Mary, one of Nancy's best friends

Eleajora, one of Orazio's lovers

About the Author

Nancy Stolfo-Corti, ne' Nancy Stolfo, is considered a Renaissance woman, because of her mastery of the ancient arts of Cooking and Wine; her accomplishment as an entrepreneur in Italian Fashion and Restaurants; and her self-taught technical sophistication in the gaming industry, software development, and internet-based media.

Nancy also has a voice that stirs hearts. She is hired to do voice-over work and narration for books by firms as prominent as the Susan G. Komen Foundation, ABC and Disney.

Nancy always felt she was a writer, but as a non-native speaker of American English, teachers were always focusing on the grammar and spelling errors that are unavoidable in a multilingual upbringing; focusing on the mistakes instead of the beautiful evocative ideas and phrasings that are natural to this first generation Italian American woman.

Nancy was a fashion designer in Florence Italy by the age of 21, doing shows in Paris, Rome and London. She is an award-winning restaurateur (Donna In Cucina, 1996, Associazione Gastronomica Italiana) and she was one of the first American women to complete the three year AIS (Associazione Sommelier Italiana) Sommelier certification.

History

The second eldest of the four Stolfo children of Rinaldo and Anna, Nancy grew up in Dayton, Ohio with occasional visits to the south of Italy where her mother was from and the north of Italy where her father was from. Her father and mother did not even speak the same language; Italian dialects can be near impossible to understand. Her mother was a seamstress and her father a baker who rose to pre-eminence becoming the President of the National Bakers Association.

From an early age Nancy read, wrote and spoke for her immigrant parents, giving her years of experience in the role of a negotiating adult before she reached 16. She studied in London at a preeminent fashion design school and landed in Florence to start her career as a designer.

In Florence during the Fall Wine season, Nancy met and fell in love with a handsome and passionate Florentine, Orazio Corti. Nancy's Italian was limited and Orazio spoke no English; theirs was the language of love. Imagine settling into a small community where Italian wasn't your native language. Imagine all the subtleties you might not catch. Imagine being considered Italian in America and American in Italy; living between worlds, fully part of neither.

Nancy and Orazio renovated a historic home and began a family in a valley in Tuscany's wine country, on the hillside where Machiavelli, the famous Italian Medieval thinker, writer of Il Principe (The Prince) had a home. That same hill was also the location of two of the horrendous murders by *The Monster of Florence*, during the time that Nancy and Orazio lived there. All this in the background, with a young daughter and then twins.

Nancy and Orazio began a restaurant in another part of their stone villa, called *Malia,* which means "an irresistible spell or curse". It is said Malia was a little of both. They were excellent cooks, and Nancy with a flair for design and elegance, the restaurant flourished.

In time Nancy would take the children back to America to ensure they had access to all that American education and opportunity could give them. Orazio was to follow, but perhaps relocating as an immigrant and leaving behind a successful realty management and development practice would be more than most men could chose to do.

The years pass as they continued their marriage across the continents and over the Atlantic. The children spend good time in Italy with their father, good time with their grandparents in Dayton, and go to school in the outskirts of Raleigh, North Carolina.

It's now just before the end of the first decade of the 21st century, and Nancy and her husband still live in separate continents, talking almost daily through Skype, a free VOIP utility. How different from the early days in the nineteen sixties and seventies when a phone call could be hundreds of dollars in few minutes. The children have all graduated college in the United States. The great depression of the 21st century is still going on.

What tomorrow brings, we do not know, but hope, dreams and possibility are always within our reach.

ᏏᎤ The Other Side of Tuscany ᏏᎷ

Cover Design by Eli

Cover inspired by Photo by Michele Power, Nancy in the lavender fields in California, next to Michael Jackson's Neverland estate in 2009, the week he passed on.

Back Cover Photo, Nancy Stolfo Corti by David Hothersall, 2002

My thanks to writer's coach, publicist and author Anora McGaha, www.anoramcgaha.com

My thanks to my manuscript readers Sherry Stolfo, Amy Martin, Mary Flannigan, Carolynn Woods, Lisa Brough, Robert Roy and Lenora Tickle.

Support and counsel from my parents, my siblings, my husband and my friends, too numerous to name here, but always dear in my heart.

For inquiries email info@nancystolfocorti.com or contact Anora McGaha, MALD at ClearSight Creative Resources, 828.398.0390.

The Other Side *of* TUSCANY

The Other Side of TUSCANY will move your heart and stir your soul with delight and dread, excitement and despair, and ever renewing hope and humor. Nancy's life is a dream come true with all the love, beauty and riches of the successful in world renowned Tuscan Italy.

Yet there was another side, a side you could not see...

...the other side of Tuscany.

Let Nancy carry you as if you were there, seeing with her eyes, feeling with her heart, hoping from her soul, through danger and drama, passion, vision and success, across the Atlantic, in and out of the glittery world of European Fashion Design, in and out of romantic Tuscany, the story-tale romance with her husband; and always, ever the the mother to her children, and sister and daughter to her family.

Nancy Stolfo Corti is a Renaissance woman who lives between the continents of Europe and America. Nancy has studied with the greats of Italian Fashion and pioneered marketing with state of the art gaming and software companies. A first time author, Nancy is a natural writer, gifted with passion, vision, poetry, depth, humor and insight. She is also a speaker, a voice talent, an innovative marketing expert and a pioneer stepping forth with vision into the 21st century.

www.nancystolfocorti.com

Made in the USA
Columbia, SC
19 February 2023